International Regulatory Co-operation

ADDRESSING GLOBAL CHALLENGES

This work is published on the responsibility of the Secretary-General of the OECD. The opinions expressed and arguments employed herein do not necessarily reflect the official views of the Organisation or of the governments of its member countries.

This document and any map included herein are without prejudice to the status of or sovereignty over any territory, to the delimitation of international frontiers and boundaries and to the name of any territory, city or area.

Please cite this publication as:
OECD (2013), *International Regulatory Co-operation: Addressing Global Challenges*, OECD Publishing.
http://dx.doi.org/10.1787/9789264200463-en

ISBN 978-92-64-19705-3 (print)
ISBN 978-92-64-20046-3 (PDF)

The statistical data for Israel are supplied by and under the responsibility of the relevant Israeli authorities. The use of such data by the OECD is without prejudice to the status of the Golan Heights, East Jerusalem and Israeli settlements in the West Bank under the terms of international law.

Photo credits: Cover © Jörg Vollmer - Fotolia.com

Corrigenda to OECD publications may be found on line at: *www.oecd.org/publishing/corrigenda*.

Foreword

This report responds to the request of the OECD Regulatory Policy Committee (RPC) to do a stocktaking exercise on International Regulatory Co-operation (IRC). It provides an overview of recent trends, the range of existing regulatory co-operation mechanisms (and actors involved) and preliminary lessons learnt from selected experiences. It builds on 10 case studies, a review of the literature and answers by RPC delegates to a questionnaire on IRC undertaken by the Secretariat in 2012.

This report is complemented by three volumes of case studies. They cover a vast range of sectors and experiences: Canada-U.S. Regulatory Cooperation Council (provided by Canada's Regulatory Cooperation Council Secretariat); chemical safety (provided by the OECD Environment, Health and Safety Division); consumer product safety (provided by the OECD Information, Communications and Consumer Policy Division); co-ordination of Bilateral Tax Treaties/the OECD Model Tax Convention (provided by the OECD Centre for Tax Policy and Administration); competition law enforcement (provided by the OECD Competition Division); transnational private regulation (developed by Fabrizio Cafaggi, Andrea Renda and Rebecca Schmidt in the framework of the Hague Institute for the Internationalisation of Law Project); as well as transboundary water management; prudential regulation of banks, EU energy regulation, and global risk assessment dialogue (all four developed by Julia Black of the London School of Economics and Political Science).

Four studies directly build on the experience of the OECD as a platform for regulatory co-operation (in the areas of chemical safety, competition law enforcement, co-ordination of bilateral tax treaties and consumer product safety). One is transversal and focuses on transnational private regulation, and another on a generic, umbrella regulatory partnership between Canada and the United States. These case studies have sought to capture the main characteristics of selected IRC experiences and follow a common structure to ensure comparability of approach.

By end 2012, 25 members had responded to the OECD IRC Survey: Australia, Belgium, Canada, Chile, Czech Republic, Denmark, Estonia, the European Union (EU), France, Germany, Hungary, Ireland, Island, Israel, Japan, Korea, Mexico, New Zealand, Poland, Slovenia, Spain, Sweden, Switzerland, the UK and the United States. The survey included three components: governments' approach to IRC, types of IRC mechanisms used, and countries' perception of benefits and challenges associated with IRC. From the answers collected by the Secretariat, completing the questionnaire has proved to be a difficult task, reflecting the lack of a consensus on some of the language used in relation to IRC and the diffused nature of IRC responsibilities – many respondents mentioned that the information on IRC was not centralised in a single place but was dispersed among line ministries and public agencies, making it time consuming and resource intensive to answer the questionnaire in a comprehensive manner. In EU countries, answering the survey was also difficult due to many IRC mechanisms common at the EU level. The answers received nevertheless proved useful for developing this report, which reflects the main survey results.

This work on IRC has been conducted under the supervision of the OECD Regulatory Policy Committee whose mandate is to assist both members and non-members in building and strengthening capacity for regulatory quality and regulatory reform. The Regulatory Policy Committee is supported by staff within the Regulatory Policy Division of the Public Governance and Territorial Development Directorate.

The OECD Public Governance and Territorial Development Directorate's unique emphasis on institutional design and policy implementation supports mutual learning and diffusion of best practice in different societal and market conditions. The goal is to help countries build better government systems and implement policies at both national and regional level that lead to sustainable economic and social development. The directorate's mission is to help governments at all levels design and implement strategic, evidence-based and innovative policies to strengthen public governance, respond effectively to diverse and disruptive economic, social and environmental challenges and deliver on government's commitments to citizens.

Acknowledgements

This report was drafted and co-ordinated by Céline Kauffmann, Senior Economist, under the supervision of Nick Malyshev, Head of the OECD Regulatory Policy Division. Excellent research assistance was provided by Philipp Beiter. This report draws on a set of case studies prepared by the OECD Environment, Health and Safety Division (on chemical safety); the OECD Competition Division (on competition enforcement); the OECD Information, Communications and Consumer Policy Division (on consumer product safety); the OECD Centre for Tax Policy and Administration (on the model tax convention); the Canada-U.S. RCC Secretariat (on the Canada-U.S. Regulatory Cooperation Council), as well as leading academics: Julia Black (on the prudential regulation of banks; transboundary water management; EU energy regulation; and global risk assessment dialogue); Fabrizio Cafaggi, Andrea Renda and Rebecca Schmidt (on transnational private regulation). Helge Schroeder co-ordinated the IRC survey answers with OECD countries.

A steering group comprising Canada, Mexico and France was established to guide the work on the topic. Canada, Mexico, and the United States provided substantive inputs on the Regulatory Cooperation Council (RCC) and on the High-Level Regulatory Cooperation Council. Other essential inputs were received from the IRC Survey respondents. Useful comments and suggestions were provided by countries of the steering group, as well as New Zealand and the United States.

Special thanks go to Julia Black, professor of law at the London School of Economics and Political Science, for her inputs throughout the development of the report, to Jeff Heynen, policy advisor in the Canadian Secretariat of the Canada-U.S. Regulatory Cooperation Council and to Fabrizio Cafaggi, professor of comparative law, for their extensive comments on the first draft of the report; to Rolf Alter, Nick Malyshev and Greg Bounds of the OECD Public Governance and Territorial Development Directorate for their useful guidance and support; and to OECD colleagues for constructive comments (in particular Richard Sigman, Antonio Capobianco, Hilary Jennings, Ewelina Marek, and Jacques Sasseville). The report was skilfully prepared for publication by Jennifer Stein.

Table of contents

Tables

Figures

Acronyms and abbreviations

ACER	Agency for the Cooperation of Energy Regulators
ANZCERTA	Australia New Zealand Closer Economic Relations Trade Agreement
ANZTPA	Australia New Zealand Therapeutic Products Agency
APEC	Asia-Pacific Economic Cooperation
ARSO	African Organization for Standardization
ASEAN	Association of Southeast Asian Nations
CABs	Conformity Assessment Bodies
CARICOM	Caribbean Community
CEN	European Committee for Standardisation
CENELEC	European Committee for Electrotechnical Standardisation
CER	Closer Economic Relations
COMESA	Common Market for Eastern and Southern Africa
COPANT	Pan American Standards Commission
EC	European Commission
ENTSOs	Energy Network Transmission System Operators
ETSI	European Telecommunication Standardisation Institute
EU	European Union
FAO	Food and Agriculture Organisation
FSANZ	Food Standards Australia and new Zealand
GHTF	Global Harmonisation Task Force
GTIN	Global Trade Item Numbers
HLRCC	High-Level Regulatory Cooperation Council
IAF	International Accreditation Forum
IAIS	International Association of Insurance Supervisors

IASB	International Accounting Standards Board
ICAO	International Civil Aviation Organization
ICPEN	International Consumer Protection and Enforcement Network
IEC	International Electronic Commission
IGO	Intergovernmental Organisation
ILAC	International Laboratory Accreditation Cooperation
ILO	International Labour Organisation
IMDRF	Medical Device Regulators Forum
IMO	International Maritime Organization
IOSCO	International Organization of Securities Commissions
IRC	International Regulatory Co-operation
ISO	International Organization for Standardization
ITU	International Telecommunications Union
MAD	Mutual Acceptance of Data
MERCOSUR	Southern Common Market between Brazil, Argentina, Paraguay, Uruguay and Venezuela
MRA	Mutual Recognition Agreement
NAFTA	North American Free Trade Agreement
NARIC	National Academic Recognition Information Centres
NIA	National Interest Analysis
NRAs	National Regulatory Authorities
NTM	Non-tariff measures
OIRA	Office of Information and Regulatory Affairs
OMB	Office of Management and Budget
OSCE	Organisation for Security and Co-operation in Europe
PIC/S	Pharmaceutical Inspection Cooperation Scheme
RPC	Regulatory Policy Committee
RTAs	Regional Trade Agreements
SAFA	Sustainability Assessment of Food and Agriculture systems
SEM	Single Economic Market
TBT	Technical Barriers to Trade
TPR	Transnational Private Regulation
TTMRA	Trans-Tasman Mutual Recognition Agreement

UNECE	UN Economic Commission for Europe
UNSCC	United Nations Standards Coordinating Committee
WAEMU	West Africa Economic and Monetary Union
WHO	World Health Organization
WTO	World Trade Organization

Preface

In an increasingly globalised world, the way the rules of the game for business, investment and trade are designed and enforced is of critical importance for the performance and competitiveness of countries. Traditionally, rules and their application are a matter of domestic competence. However, dealing with climate change, human health and safety, migration and a range of other global policy issues requires that regulators look beyond their national borders to address interconnected and cross-jurisdictional challenges. The ongoing financial and economic crisis has provided ample illustration of the dramatic impact of poor articulation and inadequate enforcement of regulation across borders.

International Regulatory Cooperation: Adressing Global Challenges highlights the gains that can be made through greater international coordination of rules and their application. The potential for cooperation in this field is significant, and its effect on improving the functioning of markets, reducing costs, helping manage global risks and creating substantial benefits for business and the public at large are likely to be huge. However, there is little structured guidance on how to promote succesful cooperation at the global level at a time when businesses and citizens require more than ever the elimination of unnecessary regulatory divergences across countries.

Evidence of the effects of better rules for globalisation is rather patchy. For example, it is recognised that thanks to the OECD Mutual Acceptance of Data system, OECD governments and industry save approximately EUR 153 million per year through reduced chemical testing and the harmonisation of chemical safety tools and policies across jurisdictions. Similarly, the Montreal Protocol on Substances that Deplete the Ozone Layer is considered one of the most successful multilateral treaties in the history of the United Nations, leading to the reduction of over 97% of all global consumption of controlled ozone depleting substances. However, international regulatory cooperation is still limited, and there is also scarce structured and systematic evidence from past experiences of how the various mechanisms for international regulatory cooperation perform in different sectors and countries.

International Regulatory Cooperation: Adressing Global Challenges is a unique attempt to gather synthetically the knowledge and evidence available to date on the various mechanisms which governments can use to promote more consistent and coordinated rules. It builds on ten case studies of regulatory cooperation in sectors as varied as competition enforcement, chemical safety, transboundary water management and prudential regulation of banks, as well as a unique survey of OECD countries. The report lays the groundwork for more informed discussions and decision-making on the ways countries and stakeholders can promote greater cooperation in rule-making and enforcement, providing concrete foundations to implement the OECD Council *Recommendation on Regulatory Policy and Governance.*

However, a lot remains to be done to promote successful regulatory cooperation. Following this seminal work, countries and international organisations should document more systematically their experience with international regulatory cooperation and collect quantitative and qualitative evidence on various cooperation mechanisms. The OECD stands ready to support their efforts and to provide a platform for informed discussions on the rules needed for an increasingly globalised world.

Angel Gurría,

OECD Secretary-General

Executive summary

With the progressive emergence of an open, dynamic and globalised economy, the internationalisation of rules has become a critical issue. Governments increasingly seek to maximise the benefits of globalisation for national populations by eliminating unnecessary regulatory divergences and barriers, and ensuring greater co-ordination of regulatory objectives. At the same time, intensification of global challenges, such as those pertaining to systemic risks (financial markets), the environment (air or water pollution), and human health and safety, is leading to growing regulatory co-operation efforts as a key component of risk management strategies across borders. Regulatory co-operation is not a new topic (OECD, 1994). However, renewed attention has been paid to its importance since the economic crisis began in 2008. Perceived regulatory failures related to poor articulation of regulation across borders, limited enforcement of rules and regulatory capture have raised questions regarding the role of the state as a regulator and, specifically, how and where it should intervene to achieve key policy objectives in an increasingly globalised world.

The gains that can be achieved through greater co-ordination of rules and their application across jurisdictions remain largely untapped and under-analysed. Consensus has grown among countries over the years on the elements of "good" regulation at domestic level, culminating in 2012 with Council's approval of the Recommendation on Regulatory Policy and Governance. By contrast, the potential of international regulatory co-operation (IRC) to transfer good regulatory practices, to make markets function better, to level the playing field, to reduce costs, to manage global goods and risks better and to generate substantial benefits for business and the public has not been explored systematically. Despite its potential and the fact that the OECD and others have accumulated a large body of experience in fostering regulatory co-operation in a number of specific areas, including environment, competition, consumer protection and tax, this vast body of (mostly qualitative) knowledge has yet to be synthesised and analysed to provide useful lessons.

This report is a unique attempt to gather in a synthetic but systematic manner, the knowledge and evidence available to date on IRC. This report reviews the available evidence on IRC drawn from a literature review, a survey to OECD countries and case studies of specific IRC experiences and lays the foundation for further work on IRC. Chapter 1 systematically defines and documents a wide range of IRC mechanisms and highlights a number of prevailing trends in the internationalisation of regulation, laying the foundation for the development of a typology. Chapter 2 reviews the benefits, challenges and costs of IRC and highlights the critical conditions of success, laying the foundations for the development of a checklist to support governments' efforts in identifying adequate forms of IRC in a specific context and in developing and strengthening successful co-operation. The areas where further work is needed are elaborated upon in the conclusion.

The review of evidence confirms the increased internationalisation of regulation, which takes place through a wide variety of IRC mechanisms and multiple actors. Today, governments use and combine a broad range of formal and informal, broad and specific IRC mechanisms to achieve their co-operation objectives. In a given policy area, there can be different forms of IRC. The strengthening of IRC is accompanied by a multiplication of state and non-state actors with regulatory powers, i.e. different levels of government and public agencies and private national and international stakeholders. As a result, countries are embedded in webs of regulatory co-operation that go beyond the traditional treaty-based model of international relations, to encompass transgovernmental networks involving multiple actors with sometimes limited oversight or monitoring by the centre of government.

To keep pace with the need to regulate across borders, the nature of IRC has changed from complete "harmonisation" of regulation (i.e. uniformity of laws) to more flexible options – such as mutual recognition agreements. This shift is partly due to the recognition that frictions generated by regulatory divergences result as much from diverging enforcement and implementation efforts as from differences in the regulations and standards themselves. Consequently, harmonisation of rules will address only one aspect of regulatory divergences. The understanding that regulatory co-operation needs to encompass all phases of the policy cycle is growing and with it the recognition that flexible mechanisms need to be put in place to address implementation challenges and to anticipate forthcoming issues. In this context, soft law and informal co-operation – such as dialogue between regulators and exchange of information – are becoming more important in promoting regulatory co-operation, generally in support or in anticipation of more binding processes, and as a flexible tool to address emerging global issues. Similarly, the trend is towards the development of supporting international organisations that provide a platform for continuous discussions.

Despite growing regulatory co-operation, decision making on IRC remains mainly guided by political considerations and is not informed by a clear understanding of benefits, costs and success factors of the diverse IRC options. In some areas, co-operation has led to obvious successes. Experience accumulated in chemical safety, for example, shows that the use of harmonised approaches and instruments leads to important savings for governments and industries, while allowing greater achievement of public policy objectives. Most cases of successful co-operation have, however, tended to develop in an ad hoc manner, along "paths of least resistance", and without following general principles of good regulatory governance. There is no overall and cross-country consensus yet on the language used in relation to IRC, or on the range and definition of the different mechanisms in the hands of policy makers to promote IRC. The quantitative evidence on the benefits and costs of IRC remains scant. Changing language and anecdotal evidence generate uncertainty with regards to the benefits and costs of regulatory co-operation and prevent systematic and rational decision making on IRC.

The shortcomings and gaps in policy making related to IRC call for further analytical work and guidance for which the OECD Regulatory Policy Committee is well positioned to provide useful inputs. While most countries acknowledge the importance and potential value of IRC, very few have started considering and mainstreaming issues of international co-operation into their regulatory process. More could be done in support of country efforts to identify the range of existing IRC mechanisms, to assess the benefits, costs and challenges of IRC in specific sectors and situations, and to strengthen IRC following good regulatory policy principles. Similarly, the emergence of new actors with regulatory powers on the international scene has been mostly spontaneous, and has not necessarily been matched with corresponding good regulatory practices. As an example, while transnational private regulation plays a growing role, governments have limited systematic tools at their disposal to evaluate when and under which conditions transnational private regulation might be a preferable regulatory option. Similarly, while international organisations play a growing role in supporting IRC, the extent to which they do so while following good regulatory policy practices is unclear.

Chapter 1

Trends in international regulatory co-operation

This chapter is a unique attempt to synthesise the knowledge and evidence available to date on the various mechanisms used by governments to promote regulatory co-operation. It first identifies 11 IRC mechanisms and provides evidence on the frequency of their use by governments. It then reviews the trends in IRC over the past decades. The review of evidence confirms the increased internationalisation of regulation, which takes place through a wide variety of mechanisms and multiple actors. It highlights a shift in the nature of IRC from complete "harmonisation" of regulation to more flexible options – such as mutual recognition agreements.

In the early 1990s, OECD (1994) highlighted the internationalisation of regulation, noting that "Regulatory actors and processes are crossing national, regional, and local borders, with initial caution but increasing confidence, to share information and ideas, and to co-ordinate the design, analysis, drafting, and enforcement of regulations". This trend has been confirmed in the 20 years that followed as illustrated by a series of indicators used in OECD (1994) and updated to recent years (see figures 1.1 and 1.2). The rapid expansion of globalised approaches to economic regulation "has been accompanied by correspondingly rapid institutional innovation" (as reported by Levy, 2011) and combines a diverse array of participants and of approaches to rulemaking. This is reflected in the widening range of IRC mechanisms – formal and informal, broad and specific – that governments use and combine to co-operate. This chapter precisely seeks to identify, define and analyse the different forms of IRC, the frequency of their use and the major changes that have occurred in the past decades in the way regulatory co-operation is being achieved.

Figure 1.1. OECD Council instruments

(cumulative numbers, as of end 2012)

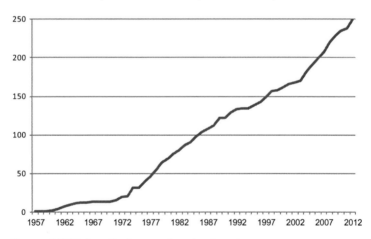

Source: OECD, http://webnet.oecd.org/oecdacts/.

Figure 1.2. Number of ISO standards published

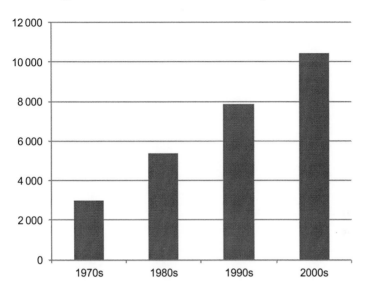

Source: ISO Catalogue, www.iso.org/iso/fr/home/store/catalogue_ics.htm, accessed 01/12/2011.

The widening range of IRC mechanisms and their combination

According to OECD (1994), "practical arrangements for co-operation – articulated through a vast array of agreements, treaties and co-operative activities between various tiers of government – are so complex as to bewilder the average citizen (and not a few experts). These arrangements range from supra-national institutions (for example the European Communities [...]), through international multilateral agreements (NAFTA, the technical Barriers to Trade Agreement in the GATT, Decisions of the OECD Council), bilateral treaties and co-operative agreements (such as the Australia-New Zealand Closer Economic agreement), national-local agreements to share responsibility for making and implementing rules[...], to regulatory agreements between sub-national governments (negotiations among Canadian provinces to reduce trade barriers, regional agreements on river basins)". OECD (1994) further notes that "As a result, a web of formal and informal intergovernmental regulatory relationships is emerging in the OECD area (and beyond) that simultaneously empowers and constrains governments with respect to their ability to solve problems through regulation." This analysis is largely confirmed by the recent evidence collected in support of this work.

The range of IRC mechanisms

Despite the wide range of IRC mechanisms, a detailed typology of regulatory co-operation does not exist yet. Levy (2011) notes that the rapid expansion in global regulation has largely been driven from the bottom up, from practitioners experimenting with a diverse array of initiatives, generally "with little awareness of the variety of potential approaches, of ways in which their initiative fits into a broader whole". The lack of common understanding of the range of IRC options is also illustrated by the answers to the OECD IRC survey. In practice, and according to the answers, almost no country uses a single definition of IRC across all levels of government;[1] has developed a classification that groups the different IRC mechanisms in a fully comprehensive manner; nor keeps a unique, centralised database or a list of all existing IRC mechanisms (see Figure 1.10). Similarly, the literature focuses on specific arrangements but does not provide an overview of the full range of IRC mechanisms.

As a result, this report cannot rely on existing classifications to organise the information on IRC.[2] Instead, it builds on the relevant literature and information collected through the OECD IRC survey and case studies to highlight 11 different categories of IRC mechanisms. These 11 categories have been classified by order of formality and comprehensiveness (from the most formal and comprehensive to the least formal and comprehensive). They are defined and related to illustrative examples in Table 1.1. This section provides some evidence on how these various mechanisms function and the extent to which they are used by countries. While these categories represent the mechanisms most often referred to by countries and in the literature, they constitute a mix of tools and arrangements that in some cases may overlap and whose boundaries may not be clearly distinct. Developing a classification or a typology is needed and could build on these 11 categories, but goes beyond the scope of this report and will be the subject of forthcoming work.

Table 1.1. Forms of IRC mechanisms, illustrative examples and case studies

Type of mechanism	Definition	Illustrative examples and case studies
Integration / harmonisation through supra-national or joint institutions	National regulatory competences leave way to supra-national law making and institutions. Regulatory co-operation takes place primarily through harmonisation of rules.	EU institutions and directives. The joint Food Standards Australia and New Zealand (FSANZ) and the Australia New Zealand Therapeutic Products Agency (ANZTPA). Case study on EU energy regulation.
Specific negotiated agreements (treaties/conventions).	Formal forms of regulatory co-operation signed by states and binding at international law whereby each participating government agrees details of regulatory requirements, legal obligations and responsibilities on a specific topic/area. These include treaties, conventions and protocols. The agreements may be supported – or not – by a specific institution.	Multilateral (Montreal protocol); or bilateral agreements (tax treaties). The case study on transboundary water management illustrates IRC through international law supported by specific institutions, notably the Rhine Commission. The case study on the OECD Model Tax Convention illustrates the co-ordination of bilateral tax treaties.
Regulatory partnerships between countries	Formal, umbrella-type, broad political agreements between countries that they will co-operate to promote better quality regulation and minimise unnecessary regulatory divergences.	Case study on the Canada-U.S. Regulatory Cooperation Council. Other examples include the Transatlantic Economic Partnership, the Mexico-US High-Level Regulatory Cooperation Council, and the trans-Tasman co-operation.
Inter-governmental organisations	Membership in international organisations (established by treaty) promoting regulatory co-operation.	ILO, OECD, WTO, APEC among many others. The case studies on the chemical safety, the OECD Model Tax Convention and consumer product safety illustrate how the OECD works to promote co-operation among members.

Table 1.1. Forms of IRC mechanisms, illustrative examples and case studies (*cont.*)

Type of mechanism	Definition	Illustrative examples and case studies
Regional agreements with regulatory provisions	Formal regional agreements including regulatory provisions among other provisions aimed at facilitating economic and trade integration, such as regional trade agreements or economic co-operation.	The WTO database of regional trade agreements (RTAs) provides a list of RTAs in force. APEC provides an example of regional agreements with regulatory provisions.
Mutual recognition agreements (MRAs)	Principle of international law whereby States party to mutual recognition agreements recognise and uphold legal decisions taken by competent authorities in another Member State.	EU "New Approach" to technical harmonisation and standardisation (1985) Trans-Tasman Mutual Recognition Arrangement between Australia and New Zealand. The case study on chemical safety provides an example of a MRA taking place in a multilateral setting.
Transgovernmental networks	Co-operation based on loosely-structured, peer to peer ties developed through frequent interaction rather than formal negotiation involving specialised domestic officials (typically regulators) directly interacting with each other (through structured dialogues, MoUs), often with minimal supervision by foreign ministries.	International Competition Network, Basel Committee on Banking Supervision among many others. Case studies on competition law enforcement and prudential regulation of banks.
Formal requirements to consider IRC when developing regulations	Cross-sectoral and cross-government requirements imposed on responsible authorities to consider all relevant international standards and frameworks for co-operation in the same field when developing regulatory measures. When this process leads to the adoption or recognition of another jurisdiction's laws or standards, it can be assimilated to a case of unilateral co-ordination.	COAG Best Practice regulation.

Table 1.1. **Forms of IRC mechanisms, illustrative examples and case studies** (*cont.*)

Type of mechanism	Definition	Illustrative examples and case studies
Recognition of international standards	Incorporation of international standards in legislative instruments by means of a reference to one or more standards, or the replacement of entire text in the drafting of a code or regulation.	Examples include references to/or adoption of text from ISO standards and other international standard setting bodies. Case study on transnational private regulation.
Soft law	Co-operation based on instruments which are not legally binding, or whose binding force is somewhat "weaker" than that of traditional law, such as codes of conduct, guidelines, roadmaps, peer reviews, etc.	OECD set of Guidelines and Principles, combined with peer review mechanisms. Case studies on the OECD Model Tax Convention; competition law enforcement and control of chemicals.
Dialogue/Informal exchange of information	Conferences, forums and similar settings where regulators and various stakeholders from different jurisdictions meet to exchange on regulatory issues.	Transatlantic dialogues instituted by the EU and the United States through the Transatlantic Economic Council, involving Transatlantic Business Dialogues, Transatlantic Consumer Dialogues. Case study on consumer product safety and the Global Risk Dialogue.

Source: OECD elaboration based on a review of the literature, the OECD IRC Survey and the OECD IRC case studies.

Integration/harmonisation through supra-national or joint institutions

With this first IRC mechanism, national regulatory competences leave way to supra-national law making and institutions. The EU stands out as an emblematic example of harmonisation for the breadth and depth of its regulatory and economic integration. With the focus on regulation one of its defining features, the EU is referred to by some scholars as a "regulatory state" (Majone, 1996). Under the Treaty on the Functioning of the European Union, member States have ceded part of their sovereignty and empowered the EU institutions to adopt laws. These laws (regulations, directives and decisions) take precedence over national law and are binding on national authorities (see http://ec.europa.eu/eu_law/index_en.htm). The EU is supported by specific supra-national institutions (the European Commission, the European Parliament and the European Court of Justice). Other, more limited, examples of integration based on joint institutions include the Nordic co-operation and the Benelux Union (Box 1.1).

Box 1.1. The Nordic co-operation and the Benelux

The Nordic co-operation involves five North European countries: Denmark, Finland, Iceland, Norway and Sweden. It relies on the Nordic Council, an inter-parliamentary body established in 1952, the Nordic Council of Ministers, an inter-governmental body bringing together ministers from national governments in 11 policy areas established in 1971, and some 20 Nordic organisations and institutions.

The Benelux Union was constituted by a treaty between Belgium, Luxembourg and the Netherlands in 1958 for a period of 50 years. A new treaty was signed in 2008 for an indefinite duration. While the initial treaty focused on the economic union across the three countries, the new treaty is broader and involves not only issues of internal market, but also sustainable development and justice. Within the context of the EU, the Benelux Union is seen as allowing common contribution in EU instances; co-operating in the transposition of EU legislation; and going further than the EU in a number of areas.

The key institutions of the Benelux involve:

- The Committee of Ministers (*Comité de ministres*)

- A Council (*Conseil Benelux*)

- A consultative interparliamentary Council

- A court of justice to ensure the uniform application of the Benelux legislation

- A general Secretariat

The legal instruments of the co-operation include:

- Decisions by the Committee of Ministers: they are legally binding and need to be translated into national legislation

- Conventions established by the Committee of Ministers

- Recommendations by the Committee of Ministers: they are legally non-binding, but a great moral force

- Directives by the Committee of Ministers to the Council and/or the General Secretariat

Source: www.norden.org/en/about-nordic-co-operation/ and answer from Belgium to the IRC Survey.

However, despite the rapid increase in global economic integration, supra-nationalism remains the exception (Kahler and Lake, 2011). Even in the EU, where total *ex ante* harmonisation of member state national regulations was initially sought to align all member states' regulations in a given policy area, deadlocks and the realisation that full harmonisation may sometimes be too costly and a disproportionate approach compared to the market failure it is meant to address, have led to a change in the approach to focus only on harmonisation of essential requirements. In areas that do not fall under these essential requirements, the EU regulatory co-operation largely takes the form of mutual recognition agreements (see the section on MRAs below). Similarly, despite their long-standing regulatory co-operation, Australia and New Zealand note that "regulatory harmonisation can be costly and will only be the best option in some circumstances" (Australia and New Zealand Productivity Commissions, 2012). An example is the repeated attempts at harmonising regulation of therapeutic goods through the creation of a joint regulator (the Australia New Zealand Therapeutic Products Agency, ANZTPA). The Productivity Commissions of both countries note that the introduction of ANZTPA has been a long and difficult process, and one which, 13 years after its inception, has yet to be completed.

Treaties/conventions

Treaty ratification can be seen as the traditional (20th century) model of international co-operation, in which central governments are the key actors (Raustiala, 2002). Because treaties are signed by the states, information on treaty signatories and processes is easily available. The UN maintains a database of treaties and various publications that provide information on the status of the agreements (http://treaties.un.org/). Estonia, New Zealand and Australia provide examples of countries that have centralised all treaties for which the country is the signatory in a single website.[3]

Co-operation on tax matters provides a good illustration of the traditional model of IRC. As developed in the case study on the OECD Model Tax Convention, tax treaties are concluded by States (generally at federal level) and are subject to a national approval and ratification process that varies from country to country. In most countries, that process involves some form of parliamentary approval. Also, tax treaties are typically incorporated into domestic law and require interpretation by domestic courts. The case study shows that beyond the web of more than 3 500 bilateral tax treaties concluded between countries, there is value in an additional co-operation mechanism that allows some alignment in the design and interpretation of tax treaties, through internationally-agreed standards and draft provisions.

The water sector is another sector where over 250 legally binding agreements have been reached since the mid-20th century with respect to transboundary water management of individual river basins (see case study on transboundary water management). According to Wolf and Hamer (2000), most of these agreements are bilateral, but important multilateral agreements exist for the management of some significant watercourses. In addition, two Conventions set out the legal principles on transboundary water management: the 1992 Helsinki Convention (which applies to countries from the EU, Eastern Europe and Central Europe) and the 1997 UN Convention on the Law of non-Navigational Uses of International Watercourses.

Regulatory partnerships

Regulatory partnerships between countries represent forward looking joint commitments by central governments to develop permanent and lasting approaches to greater co-ordination of regulatory practices, processes, and activities. Regulatory partnerships help create general co-operation agreements to address regulatory inconsistencies and to avoid future misalignments. Although these umbrella partnerships are not treaty-based instruments and, therefore, are not enforceable under international law, their announcement by leaders and co-ordination by central agencies increase both their public visibility and their implementation by regulators. As such, however, they require the involvement of additional authorities in the completion of individual initiatives and an appropriate follow up by the co-ordinating central agencies. Prominent examples of such regulatory partnerships include the trans-Tasman co-operation (considered the oldest in this category – see Box 1.2), the Canada-U.S. Regulatory Cooperation Council, the Transatlantic Economic Partnership, and the Mexico-US High-Level Regulatory Cooperation Council.

The case study on the Canada-U.S. Regulatory Cooperation Council provides an illustration of a regulatory partnership under development. The RCC was jointly announced by the leaders of the two countries in February 2011 as an initiative between both federal governments to pursue greater alignment in regulations, to increase mutual recognition of regulatory practices and to establish smarter and less burdensome regulations in specific sectors. The RCC's initial Action Plan of December 2011 addresses four key sectors: agriculture and food; transportation; health and personal care products and workplace chemicals; and the environment; and encompasses 29 initiatives in total. Thirteen bilateral working groups involving Canadian and US counterpart agencies are responsible for implementing detailed work plans for the 29 initiatives. The RCC has a mandate to meet quarterly and to provide strategic direction to the overall initiative. As a flexible umbrella mechanism, the RCC covers a diversity of regulatory functions and forms of collaboration, which are detailed in the case study and include technical and scientific collaboration, information sharing, common application procedures, joint compliance and enforcement information, mutual recognition of testing, conformity or inspection processes, and joint standard setting.

Box 1.2. **Trans-Tasman government institutional co-operation**

Regulatory co-operation between Australia and New Zealand relies on an array of formal and informal arrangements, agreements and treaties, among which the pillars are the Trans-Tasman Travel Arrangement of 1973, the Australia New Zealand Closer Economic Relations Trade Agreement (ANZCERTA) of 1983, the Trans-Tasman Mutual Recognition Agreement of 1998 and the development of a Single Economic Market. The co-operation is supported by a high-level of political engagement involving regular meetings between the two prime ministers, as well as between key ministers. Connections are also strong across a range of government agencies.

Forms of co-operation involve various vehicles and activities, including:

- *Unilateral recognition or adoption of laws*: for instance, the recognition by New Zealand of the safety standards for electrical appliances issued in Australia.

- *Mutual recognition* through the Trans-Tasman Mutual Recognition Arrangements.

- *Staff exchanges*: the Australian and New Zealand Treasuries and Foreign Affairs Departments have longstanding secondment arrangements.

- *Joint ventures*: for example ENSIS on forestry research.

- Shared representation on boards, councils and other bodies.

- *Joint institutions:* for instance the Food Standards setting body (FSANZ), and the Australia New Zealand Therapeutics products Authority (ANZTPA).

- *Information sharing*: for instance, Australia and New Zealand Customs share intelligence on air passenger streams, and on risk and threat analysis.

- *Memorandum of understanding:* for instance between the privacy commissioners of the two countries or in relation to Business Law Co-ordination.

Source: The Australia and New Zealand School of Government (n.d.), "Arrangements for facilitating trans-Tasman government institutional co-operation", Australia Department of Finance and Administration and New Zealand Ministry of Economic Development; Australia and New Zealand Productivity Commissions (2012), "Strengthening trans-Tasman economic relations", discussion draft.

Intergovernmental organisations

A growing number of intergovernmental organisations (IGOs) "appear to be engaging in legislative or regulatory activity" according to Braithwaite and Drahos (2000) and Alvarez (2005). Based on the answers to the OECD survey, countries are members of a great variety of international organisations that more or less promote regulatory co-operation. In fact, most countries belong to 50 or more international organisations. The IGOs promoting some form of regulatory co-operation mentioned repeatedly by countries include the World Trade Organization (WTO), the OECD, and various United Nations (UN) bodies including the International Maritime Organization (IMO). Regional forums of a cross-sectoral nature include notably APEC and the UN Economic Commission for Europe (UNECE). Sector or area specific forums include worldwide organisations such as the International Labour Organisation (ILO), the Food and Agriculture Organisation (FAO), the World Health Organization (WHO), the International Civil Aviation Organization (ICAO) or regional organisations such as the International Commission on Civil Status, the Organization for Security and Co-operation in Europe (OSCE). Table 1.2 provides insights into the regulatory co-operation mandate of a number of these IGOs.

Table 1.2. Selected IGOs and regulatory co-operation

	Mandate in relation to regulatory co-operation
APEC	Launched in 2010 the ARCAM (APEC Regulatory Cooperation Advancement Mechanism) on Trade-Related Standards and Technical Regulations is a process through which trade officials, relevant regulators and other stakeholders conduct work on emerging regulatory issues that have relevance to APEC's agenda to strengthen regional economic integration. The purpose of this work is to develop a shared understanding of relevant issues, increase transparency and promote better alignment of technical requirements and standards. APEC's regulatory co-operation covers areas such as harmonising standards for the digital economy, common standards for life sciences research and standardised safety testing of electronic equipment and toys. www.apec.org
FAO	The Food and Agriculture Organisation is an intergovernmental organisation aimed at promoting food security through a collaborative platform. www.fao.org
IAEA	The International Atomic Energy Agency is a UN intergovernmental agency dealing with co-operation in the nuclear field. The Statute of the agency outlines three pillars of its work: nuclear verification and security, safety and technology transfer. www.iaea.org
ICAO	The International Civil Aviation Organization is a UN intergovernmental agency that promotes the safe and orderly development of international civil aviation. It sets standards and regulations necessary for aviation safety, security, efficiency and regularity, as well as for aviation environmental protection. www.icao.int

Table 1.2. Selected IGOs and regulatory co-operation (*cont.*)

	Mandate in relation to regulatory co-operation
ILO	The International Labour Organization is the international organisation responsible for drawing up and overseeing international labour standards. It is the only 'tripartite' UN agency that brings together representatives of governments, employers and workers to shape policies jointly. www.ilo.org
IMO	The International Maritime Organization is the UN specialised agency with responsibility for the safety and security of shipping and the prevention of marine pollution by ships. www.imo.org
ITU	The International Telecommunications Union is the UN specialised agency for information and communication technologies: www.itu.int/en/about/Pages/default.aspx
OECD	Intergovernmental forum in which governments share experiences in various policy areas and develop consensus based policy recommendations supported by peer-review mechanisms. www.oecd.org
OSCE	The OSCE is the world's largest regional security organisation, offering to its 57 member States from Europe, Central Asia and North America, a forum for political negotiations and decision-making in the fields of early warning, conflict prevention, crisis management and post-conflict rehabilitation. Participating States enjoy equal status, and decisions are taken by consensus on a politically, but not legally binding basis. www.osce.org
UNECE	The UN Economic Commission for Europe is one of the five regional Commissions of the UN. UNECE's major aim is to promote pan-European economic integration through policy dialogue, negotiation of international legal instruments, development of regulations and norms and exchange and application of best practices. UNECE Working Party on Regulatory Cooperation and Standardization Policies (WP 6) provides a forum for regulators and policy makers to discuss issues such as technical regulations, standardisation, conformity assessment, metrology, market surveillance and risk management. www.unece.org
WHO	The World Health Organization is the directing and co-ordinating authority for health within the UN system. Among its core functions, it is responsible for setting norms and standards and promoting and monitoring their implementation. www.who.int
WTO	Intergovernmental forum to negotiate trade agreements, operate the system of trade rules and settle trade disputes. It operates through various councils and committees, including two that deal directly with the impact of regulation on trade: the SPS (Sanitary and Phytosanitary measures) Committee and the TBT (Technical Barriers to Trade) Committee. The World Trade Report 2012 devotes a full Chapter to "International cooperation on non-tariff measures in a globalised world", www.wto.org.

Source: Based on answers to the OECD IRC Survey and the public websites of the organisations.

Regional trade and economic agreements with regulatory provisions

Regional Trade Agreements (RTAs) are proving to be important regulatory co-operation instruments, as they may involve provisions related to competition, domestic regulation, technical standards, or transparency of rules. According to the WTO database of RTAs, of the 336 or so RTAs listed, 61 explicitly cover the topic of domestic regulation, 100 have competition provisions and 99 include provisions on technical regulations, standards, and technical barriers to trade.[4] RTAs are no longer strictly based on geographic location. They may be concluded bilaterally between two countries, between one country and a group of countries, or between regions or blocs of countries. According to the case study on competition, some RTAs have very broad and non-binding language, while others mandate the parties to prohibit very specific types of practices within their jurisdiction. Others, still, fall somewhere in between the two.

Box 1.3. Regulatory co-operation in the Unique Free Trade Agreement between Mexico and Central America

The Treaty, signed in November 2011, between Mexico, Costa Rica, El Salvador, Guatemala, Honduras and Nicaragua aims to harmonise the legal framework between the parties involved in the areas of trade of goods and services, public purchases, investment, electronic trade, intellectual property, treaty administration and dispute resolution. The Treaty includes a chapter on regulatory co-operation (Article 9.10), which covers three elements:

- *The objectives of the regulatory co-operation*, which include: *i)* to strengthen the mechanisms in support of transparency in the elaboration process of technical rulebooks, norms and conformity assessment; *ii)* to simplify the requirements provided by technical rulebooks and conformity assessment processes; and *iii)* to promote compatibility and harmonisation of technical rulebooks, norms and conformity assessment processes.

- *The establishment of a Committee* on "Technical Obstacles to Trade" is foreseen to develop the programmes for regulatory co-operation between the parts.

- *The activities on regulatory co-operation* involve, among others: the exchange of information on regulatory processes; the harmonisation and compatibility enhancement of technical rulebooks and norms; the development of mechanisms for technical assistance between the parts; the possibility of involving the other parts in the process of the development of new norms and regulations; improved compatibility of conformity assessment processes; the simplification of processes for accepting conformity assessment evaluations from a different country; and the possibility of international agreements between private organisms in charge of conformity assessment evaluations.

Source: www.economia.gob.mx/comunidad-negocios/comercio-exterior/tlc-acuerdos/america-latina.

Well-known RTAs with "regulatory" provisions include COMESA (Common Market for Eastern and Southern Africa), WAEMU (West Africa Economic and Monetary Union), CARICOM (Caribbean Community), ASEAN (Association of Southeast Asian Nations), NAFTA (North American Free Trade Agreement), MERCOSUR (Southern Common Market between Brazil, Argentina, Paraguay, Uruguay and Venezuela), the Andean Community (between Bolivia, Columbia, Ecuador, Peru and Venezuela), and the Asia-Pacific Economic Cooperation (APEC). In the ASEAN, the goal of the Consultative Committee on Standards and Quality is to harmonise to international standards and to develop mutual recognition arrangements on conformity assessment (Steger, 2012). Under MERCOSUR, key objectives have included harmonisation of technical regulations through regional co-operation, mutual recognition of conformity assessment procedures, and co-operation towards harmonisation of voluntary standards. The recently negotiated Unique Free Trade Agreement between Mexico and Central America provides another example of a free trade agreement involving a chapter on regulatory co-operation (Box 1.3).

Mutual Recognition Agreements (MRAs)

In international law, States party to mutual recognition agreements uphold legal decisions taken by competent authorities in another Member State. In general no regulatory convergence is implied by an MRA, i.e. there is no implication that the regulations are to be brought into alignment at any stage, though there may be exceptions to this.[5] Cafaggi (2010) distinguishes three types of MRAs depending on the regulatory function under co-operation: *i)* mutual recognition of standards; *ii)* mutual recognition of compliance techniques (where certification by one party is recognised as equivalent to certification by another party); and *iii)* mutual recognition in relation to enforcement (when judgements and arbitral awards are the subject of the MRAs). As a specific example, within the EU, MRAs provide for the mutual recognition between trading partners of test results and mandatory certificates for certain industrial products.[6] They cover products whose technical specifications are regulated (typically pharmaceuticals, medical devices, telecommunications equipment, automotive product, machinery, and electronic) and subject to mandatory certification. MRAs enable Conformity Assessment Bodies (CABs) nominated by one party to certify products for access to the other party's market, according to the other party's technical legislation.

The international community has a long history of concluding MRAs (Schmidt, 2012). Some MRAs have the status of a treaty because they are signed by states. Others may involve private parties and as such are not treaties – Schmidt (2012) mentions that this is particularly the case with agreements involving recognition of qualifications owing to the fact that professional associations within countries may be private bodies. Analysing the UN treaty database, Schmidt (2012) shows that among the MRAs involving public actors, 26 concern recognition of higher education certificates, 12 of drivers' licence, 15 of tonnage certificates and 6 of judicial and arbitral decisions. MRAs are mainly bilateral agreements, although the OECD's Council Acts related to the Mutual Acceptance of Data (MAD) provide the framework for a multilateral mutual recognition agreement on chemical safety.[7] One of the most significant bilateral agreements, involving USD 50 billion in transatlantic trade, is the US-EU MRA concluded in 1998, which covers telecommunications, medical devices, pharmaceuticals, recreational crafts, electromagnetic compatibility testing services and electrical equipment.

The OECD IRC Survey demonstrates that MRA is a widely used co-operation instrument. Of the 25 respondents, all mention using MRAs, as being part of the EU (when relevant) or for co-operation in specific sectors. Only eight respondents, however, were able to report or estimate the number of MRAs to which their country is a signatory. In particular, the EU countries were unable to estimate the number of MRAs concluded as being part of the EU. In some countries, such as Australia for example, line agencies maintain their own databases of mutual recognition agreements, making it difficult to have a comprehensive vision of all MRAs in force. Among the countries that have provided an estimate, the numbers vary significantly. On the one hand, Chile, Israel, Switzerland, Japan and Canada report between one and five MRAs. On the other hand, Mexico provides a list of 27 such agreements in sectors such as electric and electronic; measurement and calibration; toys safety; laboratory test; telecommunication; and information technology. In between, Estonia reports some 10 MRAs. Poland reports an estimate of 10 MRAs, not including those concluded under the EU. The Trans-Tasman Mutual Recognition Arrangement between the Australian Government and the Government of New Zealand provides the example of an umbrella mechanism, whose purpose is to implement mutual recognition principles relating to the sale of goods and the registration of occupations.

Transgovernmental networks

Transgovernmental (also known as transnational) regulatory networks are defined by Verdier (2009) as "informal multilateral forums that bring together representatives from national regulatory agencies or departments to facilitate multilateral co-operation on issues of mutual interest within the authority of the participants". They have emerged in the second half of the 20th century to complement the traditional treaty-based approach to regulatory co-operation in areas such as securities regulation, competition policy, and environmental regulation. Raustiala (2002) finds that agencies that in the past rarely considered the international sphere, are now actively co-operating with their foreign counterparts in matters of enforcement, policy development, capacity building and information sharing. This collaboration is frequently guided by informal or legally non-binding agreements, and takes place through peer-to-peer collaboration, sometimes in person and sometimes virtually. These networks may be supported by a lead organisation (IOSCO), or not (International Competition Network). Co-operating directly with peers in other jurisdictions permits government officials to maximise their ability to fulfil their domestic mandates and enforce domestic law more effectively. Transgovernmental networks facilitate the convergence of domestic regulation without necessarily implying the centralisation of rulemaking, although in some cases, such as in banking supervision, they do develop codes and rules that members are expected to implement in national law.

Because these networks are multiplying fast, drawing up an exhaustive list is difficult. Transgovernmental networks also vary widely in their constituency, governance structure and operational mode. Box 1.4 provides some examples.

Box 1.4. Selection of transgovernmental networks

The **European Public Administration Network** is an informal network of the Directors General responsible for Public Administration in the Member States of the EU whose mission is to improve the performance, competitiveness and quality of European public administrations by developing new tools and methods in the field of public administration: www.eupan.eu/en/content/show/&tid=188.

The **Basel Committee on Banking Supervision** provides a forum for regular co-operation on banking supervisory matters: www.bis.org/bcbs.

The **International Organization of Securities Commissions** (IOSCO) gathers agencies committed to co-operate in developing, implementing and promoting adherence to internationally recognised and consistent standards of regulation, oversight and enforcement in order to protect investors, maintain fair, efficient and transparent markets, and seek to address systemic risks: www.iosco.org.

The **International Association of Insurance Supervisors** (IAIS) represents insurance regulators and supervisors of some 190 jurisdictions and issues global insurance principles, standards and guidance papers, organises meetings, provides training and support on issues related to insurance supervision: www.iaisweb.org.

The **International Consumer Protection and Enforcement Network** (ICPEN) is composed of consumer protection authorities from 40 countries, whose aim includes to share information about cross-border commercial activities that may affect consumer welfare and encourage global co-operation among law enforcement agencies: https://icpen.org.

Box 1.4. **Selection of transgovernmental networks** (*cont.*)

The International Competition Network provides competition authorities with a specialised yet informal venue for maintaining regular contacts and addressing practical competition concerns: www.internationalcompetitionnetwork.org.

The **International Laboratory Accreditation Cooperation** (ILAC) is an international co-operation of laboratory and inspection accreditation bodies formed to help remove technical barriers to trade: www.ilac.org/home.html.

The **International Accreditation Forum** (IAF) is the world association of Conformity Assessment Accreditation Bodies and other bodies interested in conformity assessment in the fields of management systems, products, services, personnel and other similar programmes of conformity assessment: www.iaf.nu.

The **Pharmaceutical Inspection Cooperation Scheme** (PIC/S) facilitates the networking between participating authorities and the maintenance of mutual confidence, the exchange of information and experience in the field of good manufacturing practices and the mutual training of GMP inspectors: www.picscheme.org/pics.php

The **Strategic Approach to International Chemicals Management** (SAICM) was adopted in 2006 by over 100 governments to foster the sound management of chemicals and ensure that by 2020, chemicals are produced and used in ways that minimise significant adverse impacts on the environment and human health: www.saicm.org.

Until 2012, the **Global Harmonisation Task Force** (GHTF) was a partnership between regulatory authorities and regulated industry to achieve greater uniformity between national medical device regulatory systems, comprised of five Founding Members (EU, United States, Canada, Australia and Japan). Following its dissolution, the **International Medical Device Regulators Forum** (IMDRF) was launched in February 2012 to discuss future directions in medical device regulatory harmonisation. It is a voluntary group of medical device regulators from around the world who have come together to build on the strong foundational work of the GHTF, and to accelerate international medical device regulatory harmonisation and convergence: www.ghtf.org and www.imdrf.org.

The **European Network of National Information Centres on academic recognition and mobility** (ENIC) was established by the Council of Europe and UNESCO to implement the Lisbon Recognition Convention. The Network of **National Academic Recognition Information Centres** (NARIC) was created by the European Commission in 1984 to improve mutual academic recognition of diplomas and periods of study in EU countries, the European Economic Area countries and Turkey. In each participating country, a specific office (generally the same office for both networks) was designated by the ministries of education, but with varying status and scope of work. Mostly, ENIC-NARICs offer information and advice on foreign education systems and qualifications. They also interact informally on issues of common interest, such as the evaluation of specific degrees from other countries: www.enic-naric.net.

Source: Based on answers to the OECD IRC survey and websites of the organisations.

Formal requirements to consider all relevant frameworks for co-operation in other jurisdictions

The *2012 OECD Recommendation of the Council on Regulatory Policy and Governance* recommends that members "in developing regulatory measures, give consideration to all relevant international standards and frameworks for co-operation in the same field and, where appropriate, their likely effects on parties outside the jurisdiction". This recommendation notably requires that governments take into account relevant international regulatory environment when formulating regulatory proposals; act in accordance with their international treaty obligations; and avoid the duplication of efforts in regulatory activity in cases where recognition of existing regulations and standards would achieve the same public interest objective at lower costs. This form of IRC can be assimilated to a case of "unilateral harmonisation" as described by Meuwese (2009) or of "unilateral co-ordination" as defined by the Policy Research Initiative (2004), whereby countries take unilateral steps to co-ordinate their regulatory approaches with other jurisdictions.

Ex ante consideration of regulatory co-operation provides a powerful way to prevent the development of future incompatibilities. Indeed, according to Urpelainen (2009), "If states intervene early to harmonise regulations and co-ordinate the development of domestic regulatory institutions, they benefit in two ways. First, low adjustment costs facilitate bargaining. Second, the co-ordinated development of domestic regulatory institutions creates a beneficial lock-in that reduces the incentive to deviate in the future".

In an attempt to evaluate whether countries apply such a principle, the OECD IRC survey included the following question: "When developing regulatory measures, is there a formal cross-sectoral requirement to consider all relevant frameworks for co-operation in other (foreign) jurisdictions in the same field?". Figure 1.3 illustrates the answers provided by countries. The answers show that among the respondents, roughly one third have a formal cross-sectoral requirement; eight have a sector by sector approach; and nine have no formal requirement at all. However, while there is a formal requirement in some countries, there is little homogeneity in the way it is implemented. Box 1.5 provides an illustration of how Australia, Canada and the United States consider IRC in their regulatory processes.

Figure 1.3. Requirement to consider all relevant frameworks for co-operation in other (foreign) jurisdictions in the same field

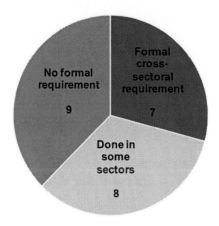

Source: OECD (2012), Survey on International Regulatory Co-operation.

Box 1.5. **How is IRC taken into account in the regulatory process of Australia, Canada and the United States**

In **Australia**, there is a cross-sectoral requirement to consider "consistency with Australia's international obligations and relevant international accepted standards and practices" (COAG Best Practice Regulation). Wherever possible, regulatory measures or standards are required to be compatible with relevant international or internationally accepted standards or practices in order to minimise impediments to trade. National regulations or mandatory standards should also be consistent with Australia's international obligations, including the GATT Technical Barriers to Trade Agreement (TBT Standards Code) and the World Trade Organization's Sanitary and Phytosanitary Measures (SPS) Code. Regulators may refer to the Standards Code relating to ISO's Code of Good Practice for the Preparation, Adoption and Application of Standards.

The Treasury Board of **Canada** produced in 2007 Guidelines on International Regulatory Obligations and Co-operation. These Guidelines provide guidance on how to interpret the Cabinet Directive on Streamlining Regulation, which states that departments and agencies are to take advantage of opportunities for co-operation by:

- Reviewing and influencing international best practices, sharing knowledge, adopting or contributing to the development and updating of international standards and conformity assessment procedures, and developing and pursuing compatible approaches with international counterparts;

- Limiting the number of specific Canadian regulatory requirements or approaches to instances when they are warranted by specific Canadian circumstances and when they result over time in the greatest overall benefit to Canadians;

Box 1.5. **How is IRC taken into account in the regulatory process of Australia, Canada and the United States** (*cont.*)

In particular, the Guidelines encourage departments and agencies to:

- Take IRC into account throughout the entire life cycle of regulating – development, implementation, evaluation and review;

- Think strategically about how IRC can assist in achieving regulatory outcomes;

- Establish regulatory compatibility as a goal for regulators to achieve through the design of regulations and through ongoing regulatory co-operation activities with key international counterparts;

- Actively consider IRC in the ongoing management of regulatory programmes, e.g. when developing or renewing compliance and enforcement policies, technical guidelines, and procedures that are put in place to implement regulation;

- Regularly assess the effectiveness of IRC activities, determine which ones have yielded positive outcomes and make adjustments.

In the **United States**, the guidance of the Office of Management and Budget (OMB) on the use of voluntary consensus standards states that "in the interests of promoting trade and implementing the provisions of international treaty agreements, your agency should consider international standards in procurement and regulatory applications". In addition, the recent Executive Order 13609 on Promoting International Regulatory Cooperation states that agencies shall, "for significant regulations that the agency identifies as having significant international impacts, consider, to the extent feasible, appropriate, and consistent with law, any regulatory approaches by a foreign government that the United States has agreed to consider under a regulatory cooperation council work plan." The scope of this requirement is limited to the sectoral work plans that the United States has agreed to in Regulatory Cooperation Councils. There are currently only two such Councils, one with Mexico and the other with Canada.

Source: Australia COAG Best Practice Regulation Guide: www.finance.gov.au/obpr/docs/COAG_best_practice_guide_2007.pdf; Treasury Board of Canada Guidelines on International regulatory Obligations and Cooperation: www.tbs-sct.gc.ca/ri-qr/documents/gl-ld/iroc-cori/iroc-cori-eng.pdf; US OMB Circular A 119: www.whitehouse.gov/omb/circulars_a119; US Executive Order 13609: www.whitehouse.gov/the-press-office/2012/05/01/executive-order-promoting-international-regulatory-cooperation;

Recognition of international standards

Recognition and incorporation of international standards support regulatory alignment in sectors where trade is important by allowing harmonisation of technical specifications of products. Its use has been boosted by the 1994 WTO agreement on Technical Barriers to Trade, whose Article 2.4 stipulates: "Where technical regulations are required and relevant international standards exist or their completion is imminent, Members shall use them, or the relevant parts of them, as a basis for their technical regulations except when such international standards or relevant parts would be an ineffective or inappropriate means for the fulfilment of the legitimate objectives pursued, for instance because of fundamental climatic or geographical factors or fundamental technological problems".

In the EU countries, the majority of standards stems from the EU standard-setting bodies and are incorporated into national regulations. There are three standard-setting bodies at the EU level, i.e. CEN (European Committee for Standardisation), CENELEC (European Committee for Electrotechnical Standardisation) and ETSI (European Telecommunication Standardisation Institute). In order to maintain coherence and to avoid conflicts or overlaps between the European level and the international one, CEN, CENELEC and ETSI have developed special agreements with their counterparts at the international level (respectively ISO, IEC and ITU). About 21% of the CEN standards supporting EU legislation are identical to ISO standards. About 60% of CENELEC standards are identical to IEC ones. To facilitate the alignment of standards, the European standards retain the same numbering when they are identical to international standards (e.g. ISO 123 becomes EN ISO 123). Box 1.6 provides an illustration of how non-EU countries incorporate international standards in the development of national standards.

Box 1.6. Recognition of international standards in Chile and Australia

In **Chile**, Standards 2011 (NCh1), Clause No. 4.6 of the general provisions, establishes that "as a basis for the study of the Chilean standards, international standards should be taken into account (ISO, IEC, ITU, Codex Alimentarius), seeking that the deviations or amendments are minimum, except when international standards are inefficient or inadequate to achieve the desired objectives at a national level. The changes in the standards should be duly justified. In cases when international standards are not available or when they are inefficient or inadequate, regional standards should be used, and if this is not possible, national standards applied in other countries or supplementary standards that are considered adequate should be used."

In **Australia**, the Best Practice Regulation Handbook (www.finance.gov.au/obpr/proposal/gov-requirements.html#handbook) recommends that a Regulatory Impact Statement should "document any relevant international standards and, if the proposed regulation differs from them, identify the implications and justify the variations". "If any of the options involve establishing or amending standards in areas where international standards apply, you should indicate whether the standards under consideration deviate from the relevant international standards. If this is the case, you should provide an explanation for the variation and examine the implications of this variation."

Source: Based on answers to the OECD IRC Survey.

Despite the policy commitment, Fliess, et al. (2010) shows that while there is much guidance offered by various governments and standards bodies to integrate international standards in regulations, there is a clear concern that regulators are not doing enough in some sectors to incorporate international standards into regulatory documents. In particular, based on a pilot study of three sectors (domestic electrical appliances, natural gas, and telephone handsets) and five OECD members (Canada, EU, Korea, Mexico and the U.S.), the OECD reveals a lack of transparency and information on which standards are used and for which regulatory objectives, leading to a failure to produce hard evidence on the impact of international standards on trade (Fliess, et al., 2010). This is in part reflected in the answers to the OECD IRC Survey (Figures 1.4 and 1.5). Indeed, while two thirds of respondents report sectoral or cross-sectoral requirements to systematically consider recognition and incorporation of international standards in the formulation or revision of domestic standards, almost no countries were able to provide an estimate of the share of technical regulations equivalent to international standards. Among the exceptions, Mexico reports 878 technical regulations currently in force, among which 132 (15%) are equivalent to international regulations.

Figure 1.4. Requirement to consider international standards

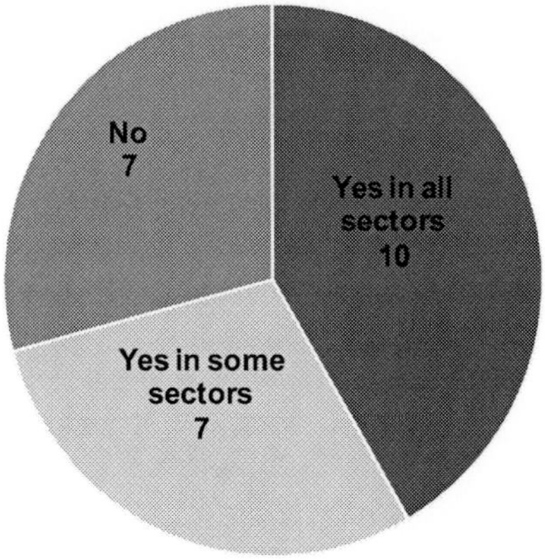

Source: OECD (2012), Survey on International Regulatory Co-operation.

Figure 1.5. Requirement to explain the rationale for diverting from international standards

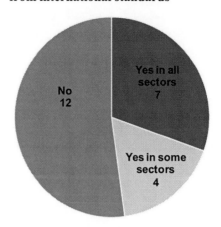

Source: OECD (2012), Survey on International Regulatory Co-operation.

Informal exchange of information

Exchange of information can help initiate co-operation in sectors where there is little common ground for co-operation (including no common language on issues to be addressed). It is difficult to track and monitor this specific mode of co-operation because, by definition, informal exchange of information does not necessarily require a formal setting to take place. However, the European Commission (EC) provides several examples of institutionalised regulatory dialogues, such as those developed with the United States, Japan, China, India and Russia (http://ec.europa.eu/internal_market/ext-dimension/dialogues/index_en.htm). Experience has shown that this mode of co-operation can be effective in problem solving and prevention in support of market opening and regulatory burden reduction for businesses operating in multiple jurisdictions.

The case study on Global Risk Assessment Dialogue is a good example of a collaboration between scientific experts in government agencies and research institutes, which occurs through international conferences organised and hosted by the EC, and multilateral working groups to address particular themes. It is expected that this low-cost form of co-operation will help build on the technical expertise of the participants to make progress in stabilising the terminology used (in risk assessments), and in the characterisations and descriptions of uncertainty. Ultimately, common understanding and terminology for expressing risk assessments and uncertainty are expected to help risk assessors to organise the information being used, clarify the weight of evidence that exists, develop consistent documentation and enhance the transparency of risk assessments, and thus facilitate the exchange of information and comparisons.

The difficulty to derive a clear-cut classification

From the preliminary list of IRC mechanisms listed in the previous section to the development of a typology that would allow sorting the tools and institutional arrangements for IRC in a way that is of operational use to countries, more work is needed. First, the 11 mechanisms described above are not mutually exclusive. Typically, several mechanisms can be used at once in the same field. Second, there are grey areas, such as IRC initiatives that share the features of several IRC mechanisms. An example is the Asia-Pacific Economic Cooperation (APEC), which is both a regional co-operation mechanism and an IGO. Another is provided by the OECD, which is an IGO promoting regulatory co-operation through soft law and exchange of information. Similarly, transgovernmental networks provide opportunities for soft law, dialogue and other forms of informal regulatory co-operation. This section illustrates these two features by analysing the layering of co-operation mechanisms and institutions, and the continuum of IRC arrangements from most to least legally binding and between public and private regulation. These two features make the development of a typology potentially a difficult endeavour and call for a refined classification that would factor in several dimensions (including the type of institutional co-operative arrangements, the instruments of co-operation, the actors involved, and the functions being co-ordinated) in order to differentiate between modes of IRC.

The layering of co-operation mechanisms and institutions

Several co-operation mechanisms can co-exist in a given area or sector of regulation and involve a variety of instruments and actors. Table 1.3 illustrates this multiplicity of forms and actors of IRC in the same field, building on information from the IRC case studies. There may be a layering of generic and specific co-operation instruments, typically through trade agreements or umbrella regulatory partnerships, as well as through specific legal instruments (treaties or other). The co-operation may involve parallel bilateral, regional and multilateral tools – such as bilateral treaties and multilateral platforms like the OECD (typically the case in tax matters) –, as well as vertical and horizontal co-operation mechanisms (e.g. network of regulators within the EU setting). Finally, most experiences of co-operation described in Table 1.3 consist of both formal and informal features.

Table 1.3. Modes of IRC and actors involved in the 10 sectors and areas of the IRC case studies

Focus	Mode of IRC	Actors involved
Chemical safety	Soft law and burden sharing through OECD: consensus-based guidance to facilitate adoption of harmonised standards (Guidelines for the testing of Chemicals, Principles of Good Laboratory Practices). Mutual recognition agreements: mutual acceptance of data in the assessment of chemicals and mutual recognition of compliance with GLP. Globally harmonised system of classification and labelling of chemicals.	OECD's Joint Meeting of the Chemicals Committee and the Working Party on Chemicals, Pesticides and Biotechnology. OECD government representatives from various ministries or agencies (health, labour, environment, agriculture, etc.), EC and selected non-members (MAD: South Africa, Slovenia, India, Argentina, Brazil, Malaysia, and Singapore). Experts from the chemicals industry, academia, labour, environmental and animal welfare organisations.
Co-ordination of bilateral tax treaties	Tax treaties. Soft law: Model Tax Convention as an internationally agreed standard for tax treaties facilitating consistent application. Dispute resolution mechanism: Manual on Effective Mutual Agreement Procedures, MEMAP.	States (federal level) for the conclusion of Tax treaties. Approval and ratification process may involve parliamentary approval. OECD. Tax officials for the development of standards.
Prudential regulation of banks	Soft law: Basel Committee standards intended to set minimum expectations: Core Principles on Banking Supervision (2006); Principles for Sharing Information between Home-Host Supervisors (2006); Basel Capital Accords: Basel I (1988, 1996); Basel II (2004, 2009) and Basel III (2010); Good Principles for Supervisory Colleges (2011). The standards are not legally binding but there is significant peer pressure for their adoption by members. Some have been enacted into law.	Financial Stability Board (government & central banks of 24 countries + BIS, BCBS, CGFS, CPSS, IAIS, IASB and IOSCO). Basel committee on banking supervision of the BIS. International Accounting Standard Board; IOSCO, IAIS. Regional bodies. Many subcommittees.

Table 1.3. Modes of IRC and actors involved in the 10 sectors and areas of the IRC case studies (*cont.*)

Focus	Mode of IRC	Actors involved
Competition law enforcement	Co-operation involves a mixture of formal and informal co-operation between different levels of government at bilateral, regional, or multilateral levels. Transgovernmental networks. Mostly bilateral co-operation between competition authorities to address anti-competitive practices. Some regional co-operation (EU). Soft law through OECD Recommendations. Dialogue: OECD Global Forum on Competition.	Centre of government for treaties. Competition authorities. OECD Competition Committee.
Consumer product safety	Voluntary co-operation that takes the form of a managed network (under OECD leadership) to co-ordinate consumer product safety initiatives. Regular meetings and exchange of information via web platforms, including the OECD global portal on product recalls.	OECD Working Party on Consumer Product Safety. Consumer agencies, national market surveillance agencies, relevant ministries, product safety regulators, standardisation bodies from OECD countries. Brazil, Egypt and India (regular observers). Indonesia, Malaysia, China, United Arab Emirates (on an *ad hoc* basis). Experts and international organisations: APEC, OAS, ASEAN, EFTA, GS1 (standard-setting body on supply-chain management), International Consumer Product Safety Caucus (ICPSC), International Consumer Product Health & Safety Organization, ISO, UNECE WP6.

**Table 1.3. Modes of IRC and actors involved in the 10 sectors and areas
of the IRC case studies** (*cont.*)

Focus	Mode of IRC	Actors involved
Water management	The legal principles are set out in a series of UN conventions, bilateral and multilateral agreements between states, in the case law of the International Court of Justice and in international customary law. Co-ordination between countries is also based on non-binding political agreements, and historical and customary use. Agreements with respect to individual river basins may be accompanied by the establishment of an institutional structure to implement the agreement.	28 UN agencies dealing with water. States in treaties and conventions. Water dedicated institutions such as the International Commission for the Protection of the Rhine.
EU energy regulation	Initially, IRC was sought through a voluntary committee of national regulators (CEER), deliberative forums on gas and electricity and voluntary agreements between national regulatory agencies, industry associations and other stakeholders. Under the Third Energy Package (2011), IRC has become more formal and is carried out through EU legislation and a set of institutions (in particular ACER). Soft law: ENTSOs codes of practice. Informal exchange of information through CEER.	Co-operative grouping of national energy regulators: Council of European Energy Regulators (CEER). EU regulatory agency: Agency for the Cooperation of Energy Regulators (ACER). Two associations of industry actors for electricity and gas: the Energy Network Transmission System Operators (ENTSOs).
Global Risk Assessment Dialogue	Dialogue and collaborative work between scientific experts in government agencies and research institutes, through: Two International Conferences on Risk Assessment, organised and hosted by the EU Commission, Five multi-lateral working groups consisting of agencies and scientists who agreed to work together on particular themes.	Initially: EU (EC, EU agencies involved in risk assessment, European Parliament); the governments of the United States and Canada. Broadened to include countries such as China, Japan, Russia, Australia and WHO. However, the range of participants narrowed between the 1st and 2nd conference to involve mainly governmental agencies of EU, United States, Canada and Australia.

Table 1.3. Modes of IRC and actors involved in the 10 sectors and areas of the IRC case studies (*cont.*)

Focus	Mode of IRC	Actors involved
Trans-national private regulation	TPR has developed as a sector specific regulation. Recently meta-private regulators have emerged which provide general rules functionally applicable to many sectors. Although TPR co-operation takes place voluntarily, it might become legally binding due to the instrument used (binding agreement, formal engagement in a regulatory organisation, etc.). Two main venues for TPR: • Organisations (association, foundation, for profit, not for profit, etc.) regulate the behaviour of their members through codes of conducts & guidelines. • Commercial contracts ensure compliance with regulation created by organisations, in particular through supply chains.	TPR is driven by multiple actors, some whose primary functions are not regulation, some regulatory organisations: firms, NGOs, independent experts, such as technical standard setters, or epistemic communities. Those actors are organising themselves in different types of private regulators: Single stakeholder (organisations) representing industries or NGOS, multi-stakeholder organisations including different actors and/or memberships categories.
Canada-U.S. Regulatory Cooperation Council	Formal (umbrella type) regulatory co-operation. Technical or scientific collaboration Information sharing Administrative streamlining Common labelling Common application procedure Joint compliance and enforcement information Mutual recognition or equivalency agreement Harmonised testing or inspection procedures Joint reference of international or 3rd party standards Joint standard setting agenda Joint regulatory development	The co-ordinating bodies for the RCC are located in the centre of government: Office of Information and Regulatory Affairs (OIRA) of the White House's Office of Management and Budget; the Treasury Board Secretariat of Canada. Other implicated bodies in the United States involve the Department of Agriculture, Department of Transportation, US Coast Guard, Food and Drug Administration, Environmental Protection Agency, and the Occupational Safety and Health Administration. In Canada, they involve the Food Inspection Agency, Agriculture and Agri-Food Canada, Transport Canada, Health Canada and Environment Canada.

Source: Based on the OECD IRC case studies, 2012.

Competition law enforcement provides a good illustration of the layering of IRC mechanisms in the same field, as it involves a mixture of competition and non-specific instruments, both formal and informal co-operation mechanisms between different levels of government. It can take place at the bilateral, regional, or multilateral levels, through international, regional and transgovernmental bodies. The different instruments and tools as well as the various types of co-operation involved in cross-border cases create a complex web of differing levels of possible engagement between authorities. Figure 1.6 provides a snapshot of these tools, which are described in the case study on competition law enforcement. While the existence of international agreements alone does not guarantee co-operation, the web of international agreements offers a formal framework for co-operation and signals a willingness to engage in a dialogue with foreign peers.

Figure 1.6. Forms of co-operation in competition enforcement

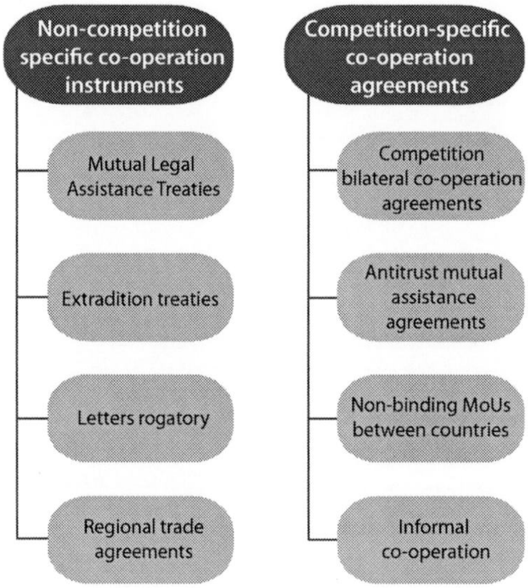

Source: Based on the case study on competition law enforcement, 2012.

Figure 1.7. Structure of global financial regulation

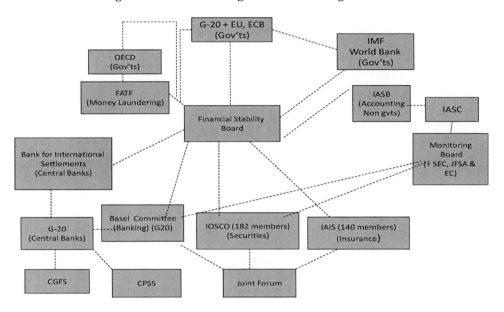

Source: Based on the case study on the prudential regulation of banks, 2012.

The multiplicity of IRC mechanisms is often combined with a multiplicity of stakeholders involved in the co-operation, as illustrated by the case study on the prudential regulation of banks. As underlined by Levy (2011), "notwithstanding the rapid globalisation of finance over the past half century – and the seemingly strong incentive to provide common regulatory rules, and a common regulatory enforcement umbrella across jurisdictions – no official global institutional arrangements have emerged that parallel the WTO. Instead, regulatory harmonisation has evolved through the seemingly *ad hoc* proliferation of inter-governmental committees (…)". As reflected in Figure 1.7, among the many actors involved, most are international committees of regulators.

There is one "supra-committee": the Financial Stability Board (FSB), formed in 2009, which comprises G20 financial regulators and finance ministers, the international committees of regulators and international organisations (the IMF, the World Bank, the European Central Bank, the EC and the OECD). The other actors are what may be termed "meta-organisations", i.e. their members are national regulators. The principal body responsible for the formation of global standards relating to banking regulation (and increasingly for their implementation) is the Basel Committee on Banking Supervision (BCBS), a sub-committee of the Bank of International Settlements. It initially comprised the G10 central banks and banking supervisors. Membership was expanded in 2009 to G20 countries. Other bodies are also engaged in this sub-sector of financial regulation, notably the International Accounting Standards Board (IASB), a non-state body of accounting professionals, and the global committees of securities regulators (IOSCO) and insurance supervisors (IAIS). The BCBS, IOSCO and IAIS co-ordinate mainly through a co-ordinating committee of the three bodies, the Joint Forum, on issues arising with respect to the supervision of global financial conglomerates which combine securities, banking and insurance activities. Collectively and individually, these bodies set a wide range of standards addressed to member state regulators concerning the regulation of financial services and markets. Under the expectations of membership, these globally agreed standards inform national regulatory standards.

The continuum of IRC mechanisms

The evidence suggests that countries combine several IRC instruments in a given area to achieve their co-operation objectives, and that IRC mechanisms are not always clearly separated, but may overlap in their features or form continuums (for example from the most to the least legally binding agreements or from public to private regulation). Figure 1.8 arranges the different IRC forms from the most constraining formal option – typically the legally binding agreements such as provided by the EU integration, treaties and other agreements binding at international law – to the least constraining ones – as provided by soft law measures such as in policy dialogues, voluntary standards, codes of conduct, and peer reviews.

**Figure 1.8. The continuum of IRC arrangements
from least to most legally binding**

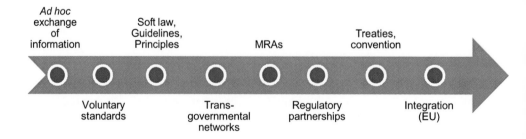

Source: OECD elaboration.

A number of grey areas exist between legally binding and non-binding agreements. Not only some non-binding agreements may be extremely powerful in their enforcement mechanisms, but there are examples of treaties and other international agreements binding in international law that have failed in their implementation due to a lack of compliance. Finally, countries may rely on a mix of binding and non-binding agreements to achieve their co-operation objectives and ensure compliance and effectiveness. For example, the case on transnational private regulation shows that although TPR usually takes place voluntarily, it might nonetheless become legally binding due to the instruments used (binding agreement such as a contract, formal engagement in a regulatory organisation, etc.). In addition, the case study argues that informality should not be associated with lower effectiveness and legitimacy. Empirical research shows that informal transnational regulatory co-operation may be highly effective and *de facto* perceived as binding. The legal dimension is only one factor that makes a co-operative agreement effective. Often market and social factors influence compliance much more than legal enforceability (Cafaggi, 2011).

The case studies on chemical safety and on the Model Tax Convention show that the binding nature of OECD instruments in practice is ensured through different means, including the adoption of provisions developed in the context of the OECD into national legislation and peer-review mechanisms. The case study on chemical safety shows that most countries adopt the OECD Test Guidelines and OECD Principles of Good Laboratory Principles into national regulations, either verbatim or with minor, non-substantive changes. With respect to national GLP compliance programmes, OECD's programme of periodic on-site evaluations of members provides for an on-site team, composed of inspectors from other OECD countries, to evaluate each Monitoring Programme every ten years. Industry is also encouraged to notify the OECD Secretariat if one country rejects a study from another country, conducted under the MAD system and to contribute to a password-protected site on issues of disharmonisation across countries in the way they implement the GLP Principles. Similarly, while not legally binding, the OECD Model Tax Convention and the OECD Transfer Pricing Guidelines can be viewed as having an intermediary status between soft law and hard law, given their role in many of the cases brought each year to court involving the application and interpretation of provisions of bilateral tax treaties and their inclusion and reference in tax treaties.

Conversely, the case study on transboundary water management highlights the difficulty in enforcing legal instruments. The 1997 UN Convention on the Law of non-Navigational Uses of International Watercourses UN Convention for instance has not yet been ratified by the required 36 countries to come into force. Even where legal agreements are in place, they may be ineffective for a number of reasons. They may be considered partial in that they relate only to certain aspects of transboundary water management, or because important riparian countries are not party to the agreement; or because the legal agreement is widely ignored and there is no effective enforcement mechanism. Wolf and Hamer (2000) for instance found that more than half of the water treaties analysed do not have monitoring provisions, two-thirds do not delineate specific allocations, and four-fifths have no enforcement mechanism.

Similarly, the distinction between public and private regulation is not always clear-cut. As shown in the case on transnational private regulation, "Private organisations" can include public members or fulfil a public mandate. Typically, ISO (a private entity under Swiss law) fulfils a public mandate. The national standard setting bodies that contribute to its work may be private, public or mixed entities. Although developed in a largely private setting, technical standards that emerge from international standard-setting bodies are incorporated into public international law documents such as the Technical Barriers to Trade Agreement. Conversely, public regulatory entities might have a high level of influential private participation. Consequently, despite the important legal implications coming from the public or private nature of the instrument of co-operation, strictly following a formalistic distinction based on the founding document and the sources of regulation (treaty, charters or bylaws, contracts or agreements) is likely to oversimplify the impact and effectiveness of such instrument.

An interesting attempt at taking into account the existence of a continuum between full public and private schemes, is provided by the "governance triangle" developed by Abbott and Snidal (2010) (Figure 1.9). This triangle allows locating governance organisations along a triangular space based on the relative prevalence of state actors, NGOs or private firms. Abbott and Snidal identify seven different "zones", corresponding to different mixes of state, NGOs and business participation. Zones 1 to 3 correspond to organisations with single actors or sets of actors, with limited cross-group participation and thus limited multi-stakeholder governance. Typically, the OECD would fall within Zone 1 because of the prevalence of the States in the co-operative arrangement. Zone 2 includes firm and industry self-regulatory schemes. Zone 3 includes codes promulgated and administered by NGOs and NGO coalitions. Zones 4 to 6 include schemes in which actors from two groups share governance responsibility (e.g. Zone 4 contains the UN Global Compact, in which civil society plays only a small role). Zone 7, the central triangle, includes institutions in which actors of all three types play a vital role e.g. ILO's Declaration on Multinational Enterprises and Social Policy.

Figure 1.9. The governance triangle

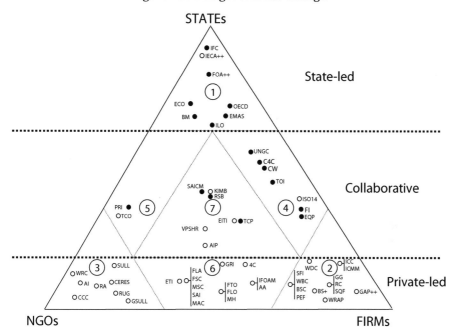

Note: Filled circles (●) are RSS schemes with direct IO participation.

Source: Abbott, K. and D. Snidal (2010), "International Regulation without International Government: Improving IO Performance through Orchestration", Vol. 5, *Review of International Organizations*, p. 315.

Recent trends: towards more flexible options

Economic integration has provided a significant driver for regulatory co-operation over the past decades. The search for a single economic market has played a critical role in the integration of the EU countries. Similarly, the co-operation between Australia and New Zealand has relied strongly on the Closer Economic Relations (CER) and the Single Economic Market (SEM). If the search for a single market for goods, services, labour and capital remains strong, the range of IRC objectives has expanded and the means to achieve these objectives have evolved over the years to accommodate the lessons learnt from early IRC experiences. The case study on EU energy regulation shows for instance that from an initial focus on economic objectives of liberalisation and the development of an efficient internal market, the objectives of EU energy policy have broadened over the last ten years to encompass environmental sustainability, security of supply, and EU solidarity. The first section also points to the multiplication of mechanisms – formal and informal, broad and specific – that governments use and combine to keep pace with the need to regulate across borders. The second section identifies two major shifts in the nature of IRC:

- A shift away from complete harmonisation of rules to more flexible regulatory co-operation mechanisms that address not only the consistency of rules but also their enforcement

- The multiplication of state and non-state actors and the rise in private regulation

The shift away from complete harmonisation of rules and the increasing use of more flexible co-operation mechanisms

The debate has moved over the years from complete "harmonisation" of regulations (involving uniformity of rules) to more flexible options that are perceived as respecting the national interest of countries and imposing less transition costs to achieve an agreement on common rules. This shift responds in part to the existence of legal constraints and inflexibilities that influence the ability of regulators to modify regulations in certain ways. It also owes to the recognition that regulatory inconsistencies may arise as much from the application of regulations as they do from divergences in the regulations and standards themselves. Typically, two countries may share the same standards and still engage in different compliance and verification efforts. The Canada-U.S. RCC provides an example where the objective is to change the administration of regulations, as opposed to their harmonisation, the latter being deemed as more time consuming and difficult, and often requiring legislative change.

The development of mutual recognition agreements (MRAs) and other instruments that preserve the regulatory power of states

In the realisation that over-harmonisation in the EU was causing poor performance of harmonisation, the Council approved in 1985 a "New Approach to Technical Harmonisation and Standardisation". Under the new approach, Community regulation is restricted to essential safety and health requirements. In the 1985 White Paper on "Completing the Internal Market" (COM(85)310 final), the EC proposed a conceptual distinction between matters where harmonisation is essential, and those where it is sufficient that there be mutual recognition of basic requirements of health and safety laid down under national law, based on the assumption that the requirements were "equivalent".

As developed in Schmidt (2007, 2012) and Nicolaïdis and Shaffer (2005), MRAs achieve a transgovernmental allocation of responsibilities with little agreement on common rules and procedures, since they rely on the competence of the different member states to regulate and enforce rules. At the heart of MRAs lies the recognition that States regulate differently to achieve equivalent aims. "Rather than agreeing on common rules and abolishing the national competence for setting them, they agree to mutually recognise products, training certificates, service standards or certification, which are all based on the rules of their home country as equivalent." Consequently, MRAs preserve the sovereign right to regulate and the national democratic accountability. At the same time, MRAs are not necessarily an easier or a low-cost option. In particular, the recognition of the simultaneous relevance of different states' rules may generate important transaction costs. This concern was addressed in the case of chemical safety through a parallel effort to harmonise the rules (e.g, via OECD Mutual Acceptance of Data scheme).

Similarly, the principle of "comity", used in enforcement of competition law (see the case study on competition law enforcement, preserves the full jurisdictional power of states while facilitating enforcement across borders. Comity is a horizontal, sovereign-state-to-sovereign-state legal principle whereby a country should take other countries' important interests into account while conducting its law enforcement activities, in return for reciprocal action. It is not the abdication of jurisdiction, but the exercise of jurisdiction with an accompanying understanding of the impact that the exercise of jurisdiction may have on the law enforcement activities of other countries. Traditional (or negative) comity involves a country's consideration of how to prevent its laws and law enforcement actions from harming another country's important interests. Positive comity involves a request by one country that another country undertake enforcement activities in order to remedy allegedly anti-competitive conduct that is substantially and adversely affecting the interests of the referring country. While, the first wave of co-operation agreements was limited to negative comity principles of avoiding harm to other countries, the 1991 EC-US Agreement, for the first time, included positive comity in the agreement on co-operation in antitrust matters. Despite being now included in many bilateral co-operation agreements between competition authorities, however, positive comity appears to have been a little-used instrument.

The supporting role of soft law and informal co-operation

Increasingly, countries resort to soft law instruments and informal dialogues to complete their battery of IRC tools. The growing role of IGOs in supporting regulatory co-operation is an illustration of this trend. Among the IGOs that promote IRC through soft law, the OECD contributes an important role. Figure 1.1 already shows the growing number of OECD Council instruments. Figure 1.10 illustrates the vast array of sectors covered by these instruments and the importance of the environment as an area of policy co-operation across member countries. OECD Council instruments include both tools that are legally binding on those member countries that do not abstain at the time of their adoption (*Decisions*) and non-binding instruments (*Recommendations*). As of end 2012, among the 249 OECD Council instruments, 28 were Decisions, 170 were Recommendations and the remaining 51 included various other instruments such as Declarations.

Similarly to other IGOs, the OECD fosters regulatory co-operation between countries by providing a platform for discussions between policy makers to meet, set standards and issue guidelines and other guidance. These discussions and tools facilitate the comparability of approaches and practices, consistent application and capacity building in countries with a less developed regulatory culture. In the tax area, the drafting of standard provisions through the OECD Council's Recommendation concerning the Avoidance of Double Taxation has greatly facilitated the negotiation and conclusion of bilateral tax treaties (see case study on the Model Tax Convention). The OECD Best Practices for Information Exchange provide guidance to competition authorities in cases where the rights of defence and legal systems differ. In the area of chemical safety (see case study on chemical safety), the OECD has played an instrumental role through three main mechanisms: *i)* consensus based guidance to facilitate the adoption of harmonised standards (Guidelines for the testing of Chemicals, Principles of Good Laboratory Practices); *ii)* mutual recognition agreements (mutual acceptance of data in the assessment of chemicals and mutual recognition of compliance with GLP); and *iii)* a globally harmonised system of classification and labelling of chemicals.

The OECD also provides member countries with flexible mechanisms to identify and adapt to new and emerging scientific areas/issues that have not been evaluated yet. For instance, in order to avoid chemical risks associated with new and un-assessed technologies and to ensure that regulatory disparities among countries are minimised and do not constitute undue trade barriers, the OECD's Chemicals Programme identifies such issues *early*, and brings policy makers together to find common solutions. With respect to nanotechnology, countries worked quickly to address the regulatory aspects of nanomaterials' safety from the beginning. The Programme has also recently initiated dialogue on the potential risks of hydraulic fracking.

Figure 1.10. OECD Council Acts by sectors

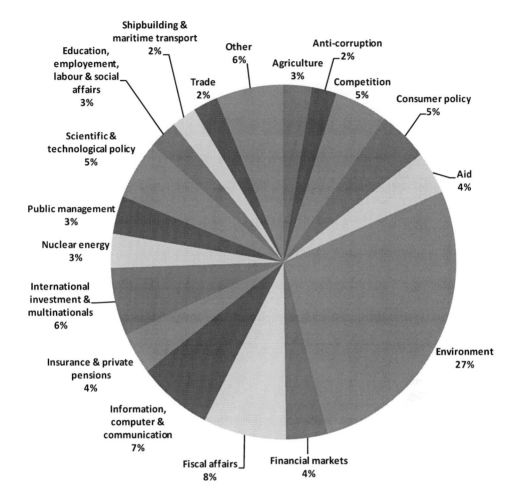

Source: OECD, http://webnet.oecd.org/oecdacts/, accessed end 2012.

At times, the OECD functions as a laboratory of co-operation experiments and lays the initial groundwork for broader international consensus. This was the case in 1984 when OECD countries agreed that the export of a hazardous chemical from an OECD country would require the importing country to be informed. This principle was laid down in the 1984 Council Recommendation, and was the basis for UNEP and FAO to develop the Rotterdam Convention on Prior Informed Consent (PIC) Procedures in

1998 (see case study on chemical safety). The Model Tax Convention provides another example of how the OECD can lay the foundation for worldwide co-operation. In 1980, the UN published the Nations Model Double Taxation Convention between Developed and Developing Countries, which was largely based on the 1977 OECD Model Tax Convention.

Informal activities of regulators at the international level, such as dialogues, complement in many instances their formal activities and help build trust and stronger foundations for more institutionalised co-operation activities (although sharing of information may be impeded by legal and other bottlenecks as highlighted in the section on challenges to IRC). For example, in the area of product safety, Australia, Canada, the EC and the United States are currently seeking to clarify and address the hazards of a number of products through dialogue, including on corded internal window coverings, baby slings and chair top booster seats. Regulators have engaged actively with stakeholders including researchers, industry representatives and consumer groups to address the problem. The newly established OECD *Ad hoc* Network of Economic Regulators (NER) provides another example of a platform supporting informal exchange of information between regulators on institutional design and regulatory practices across sectors.

The setting up of supporting international institutions

IRC is increasingly accompanied by the establishment of regional and/or international institutions with more or less regulatory powers. These institutions allow for the organic adaptation of the co-operation to new developments by providing platforms for dialogue on on-going and forthcoming co-operation issues. Such institutions may just be tasked with the management of the network of regulators to facilitate discussions (and play the role of a "network agency") or have some powers to issue rules or soft law (usually on a consensus basis) by which the members have then to abide.

Energy regulation in the EU provides a good example of where co-operation has been pursued through the setting up of network institutions, in particular a co-operative grouping of national energy regulators (the Council of European Energy Regulators, or CEER, established in 2000), a new EU-wide regulatory agency (Agency for the Cooperation of Energy Regulators, or ACER), and two approved associations of industry actors for the electricity and gas sectors (the European Network of Transmission System Operators, ENTSOs, which are by nature a form of transnational private regulation). CEER operates as a forum for the co-operation of national regulators and as an informal advisory body to the Commission (and to ACER). ACER was established in 2009 following adoption of the

"Third Package" of legislative proposals on energy to formalise the existing co-operative network of national regulatory authorities (see Box 1.7 for insights on the governance and role of ACER). ENTSOs have the task of developing Network Codes, which address cross-border issues such as network security and reliability, network connection, capacity allocation and congestion management, trading rules relating to network access, balancing, transparency, third-party access, data exchange and settlement, interoperability, and emergency operation procedures. Both ENTSOs and ACER are responsible for monitoring the implementation and impacts of the Codes.

Box 1.7. **Governance and roles of ACER**

Unusually for a European regulatory agency (but following the same model as the EU agencies for financial regulation) the ACER governance structure consists of a Board of Regulators comprised of a senior representative and one alternate of the EU Member States' 27 national regulatory authorities (NRAs) and one non-voting Commission representative. It also has an administrative board comprised of nine members and one alternate for each, of which two members (and their alternates) are appointed by the EC, two (and their alternates) by the European Parliament and five (and their alternates) by the Council. The administrative board appoints the director and is responsible for the governance of ACER, including the development of its work programme. ACER roles include:

- Ensuring the co-operation of transmission system operators (ENTSOs), who are to develop binding Network Codes, formulated in accordance with Framework Guidelines of ACER. ACER can then recommend them for adoption by the Commission through the regulatory scrutiny process, having consulted the Madrid Forum and Florence Forum.

- Approving ENTSOs' ten year plans for the development of the energy networks and their annual programmes; and monitoring progress on the implementation of projects to create new interconnector capacity

- Monitoring NRAs' implementation of the energy directives and regulations and reporting to the Commission when NRAs are do not comply with the directives or with the Agency's legally binding opinions or decisions.

- Resolving disputes with respect to access and security applicable to cross-border infrastructure when the national regulatory authorities have been unable to reach an agreement within a period of six months or they jointly request ACER to do it.

- Monitoring the internal markets in electricity and natural gas, in particular the retail prices of electricity and natural gas.

Source: Case study on EU energy regulation, 2012.

Transboundary water management is another area where co-operation has been firmly grounded in the development of co-ordination bodies. The 1992 Helsinki Convention sets out a minimum framework for agreements between riparian states based on co-operation, equality and reciprocity, good faith and good-neighbourliness. The Convention also provides that institutional structures in the form of joint bodies should be put in place to implement bi-lateral or multi-lateral agreements between riparian states. These currently include joint bodies for the management of the Danube, Elbe, Meuse, Moselle and Saar, Odura, Rhine, Aral, Chu-Talas, Lake Constance, Lake Geneva and the Saar. The International Committee for the Protection of the Rhine provides an example of a structure established to support the agreement between riparian countries of the Rhine. Box 1.8 shows the time that it has taken for such an institution to acquire credibility in an area where the preferences of members may deeply differ.

Box 1.8. The International Commission for the Protection of the Rhine

The International Commission for the Protection of the Rhine was formed in 1950 between Switzerland, the Netherlands, France, Germany and Luxemburg. It was given a legal basis by the Berne Convention in 1963. The EEC joined as a member in 1976. The Berne Convention was revised and updated by the Rhine Convention in 1999 to take into account the UNECE-Helsinki Convention of 1992, the 1997 UN Convention and the EU Water Framework Directive. Since 2000, the ICPR Member States also co-operate on an equal basis with Austria, Liechtenstein, Italy and the Belgian region Wallonia, all of which have shares in the Rhine catchment, as required under the EU Water Framework Directive.

The co-operation is taking the form of a binding international agreement, with authority delegated to the Commission by signatories, who then have to abide by Commission decisions, implement them in accordance with their national laws, and report to the Commission on implementation. The Commission has prerogatives in goal setting, supervision and monitoring areas. It is notably tasked with the preparation of programmes and studies; the co-ordination of the contracting States' warnings and alert plans for the Rhine; and the evaluation of the effectiveness of the actions decided upon. All decisions within the Commission are to be taken on the basis of unanimity.

The ICPR combines political representatives and technical experts:

- Ministers meet every 2-3 years to set common goals and agenda for the Commission.

- Senior officials meet in plenary sessions on an annual basis to determine programmes, finances and procedures.

- A co-ordination group meets four times a year and is responsible for planning and co-ordinating the work of the ICPR.

Box 1.8. **The International Commission for the Protection of the Rhine** (*cont.*)

- There are a number of permanent working groups, and individual project and expert groups on separate issues.

- The ICPR is supported by a small secretariat based in Koblenz, Germany.

- River commissions from the region have observer status in plenary sessions.

- NGOs are eligible to observe in plenary meetings and to participate in working groups as observers or experts.

Co-operation through the ICPR is broadly acknowledged as having helped improve water quality, increase the number of animal and plant species, strengthen flood prevention measures, and generally help make ecological improvements. Until 1999, however, an inadequate legal framework hampered efforts at co-ordination. In particular, the initial legal basis did not provide for rules or procedures for decision making. In addition, incongruence in preferences between upstream and downstream countries was initially not matched with a dispute resolution mechanisms and/or an agreement on the distribution of costs for prevention and remediation between the riparian states. Finally, the establishment of a common system of data collection, measurement and analysis to establish a common basis for an objective assessment of water quality has taken several decades.

Source: Case study on transboundary water management, 2012.

The multiplication of state and non-state actors with regulatory powers

The multiplication of state and non-state actors with regulatory powers reflects a change in the traditional regulatory state model, as well as a rise in private regulation.

The shift from a unitary model to multi-modal regulatory co-operation

Modern States are composed of many different constituents – different levels of government and public agencies – which have become prominent regulatory actors. These new state actors are challenging the traditional 20th century model of international co-operation based on national government representation in international organisations and multilateral treaties (as summarised in Raustiala 2002 and well-illustrated in the co-operation on tax matters, a key attribute of the centre of government). By contrast, the new actors are at the periphery of government and interact directly with their counterparts in other countries, forming what Slaughter (2000) and Raustalia (2002) call "transgovernmental networks" of regulators, with limited or no direct oversight from central governments. The rise of transgovernmental networks was facilitated by the rise of a regulatory state functionally similar across countries whereby regulators have counterparts in other countries with similar functions with whom they can discuss. It was also greatly supported by technological advances in information that made communication easier and faster. The debate on the implications of this trend for the states remains lively (Box 1.9).

Box 1.9. The pervasive role of the State

With regulatory challenges increasingly transcending national boundaries and "the golden age of the treaty [coming] to a close" (Raustiala, 2002), there is a growing perception that globalisation may have resulted in the erosion of state autonomy (Falk, 1997; Strange, 1996). However, rather than reducing the scope of state action, transnational regulation seems to increase the complexity of state interaction and the number of both state and non-state actors involved in co-operation. As Anne-Marie Slaughter noted in her article "The Real New World Order" (1997), "the state is not disappearing, [but] it is disaggregating into its separate, functionally distinct parts [...] with these parts [...] networking with their counterparts abroad, creating a dense web of relations that constitutes a new, transgovernmental order" (Slaugther, 1997).

Traditionally, the state has been seen as the predominant domestic institution to "address the adverse consequences of production, with mandatory regulation as its usual instrument" (Abbott and Snidal, 2009). On the international level regulatory co-operation has traditionally taken the form of states or groups of states setting agreements and treaties bilaterally or within international organisations. While some scholars suggest that "great power" states with large internal markets remain the key actors in writing the rules and determining the extent of regulatory policy convergence (Drezner, 2007), the multilateral, non-territorial and multi-actor modes of international regulatory co-operation today (Braithwaite and Drahos, 2000) points to a drastic evolution. Regulatory co-operation is no longer the exclusive prerogative of the nation-state. Rather, the current system seems better captured by a "governance triangle" (Abbott and Snidal, 2010) comprised of states, firms and NGOs and decentralised regulatory powers shared among private actors and state agencies. Today, even state bodies (e.g. regulatory agencies) seek to collaborate with their counterparts abroad on regulatory policy issues and form new organisational forms (e.g. Transnational Regulatory Networks, see e.g. Raustiala, 2002).

So what is left to the nation-state in this new governance era? There is a broad consensus within the scholarly literature (see e.g. Boyer and Drache, 1996; Raustiala, 2002; Abbott and Snidal, 2009) that albeit the nation-state has partly lost its exclusive prerogatives, it has by no means become obsolete but has preserved a critical, and often the decisive role in regulatory co-operation. The "regulatory state" (Majone, 1994) remains a significant player, but "as an orchestrator rather than a top-down commander" (Abbott and Snidal, 2009). When the state is not involved directly through bilateral co-operation or international organisations, it often provides the framework and necessary legitimacy for private and public-private regulatory co-operation. It does so, for instance, by setting accountability mechanisms, procedural

---

Box 1.9. **The pervasive role of the State** (*cont.*)

and substantive norms applicable to public law, minimum standards and default rules (Abbott and Snidal, 2009). The state has this prominent role in international regulatory co-operation as a consequence of its unique competencies, legitimacy, and credibility to act in the public interest, especially in the agenda-setting, negotiation and enforcement stages of regulatory policy-making at the international sphere. At times, this influence of the state in regulatory co-operation and policy-making is not even visible but operates in the background (Abbott and Snidal, 2009).

Source: OECD elaboration based on a survey of the literature, 2012.

While transgovernmental networks involve horizontal co-operation across regulators that are usually of the same level, one striking example of a co-operation that transcends levels of government is the case of the regulatory co-operation between US states, such as California, and the EU in such fields as public procurement, voluntary policy instruments and information sharing (Farber, 2011). This concerns in particular co-operation on environmental policy where both California and the EU are seen as leaders and regulatory first-movers. Vogel and Swinnen (2011) argue that California has become "a vehicle for the dissemination of European regulatory policies within the US – first at state level and lately at the federal level as well". Although American states do not have the authority to enter into formal treaties with the EU, co-operation occurs through several more informal modes (Hioureas and Cain, 2010), including Memoranda of Understanding.

The diffusion of regulatory powers across levels of government and public departments and agencies is well reflected in the answers provided by countries to the OECD questionnaire. IRC is generally not the responsibility of a single Ministry at the centre of government. It is often the responsibility of line ministries and/or public agencies in their areas of responsibility, in consultation or under the co-ordination of central/federal government ministry (typically Ministry of Foreign Affairs) when formal legal instruments are involved or when consistency of regulatory measures with international (trade or investment) agreements needs to be monitored. Because of this diffusion of IRC responsibilities, very few countries have an explicit, published policy or a law on IRC; use a unique, and agreed-to definition of IRC across all levels of government; have developed or use a classification to group the different IRC mechanisms; or keep a database or a list of all IRC mechanisms in force (Figure 1.11).

Figure 1.11. The diffusion of government responsibilities for IRC

(Number of countries with)

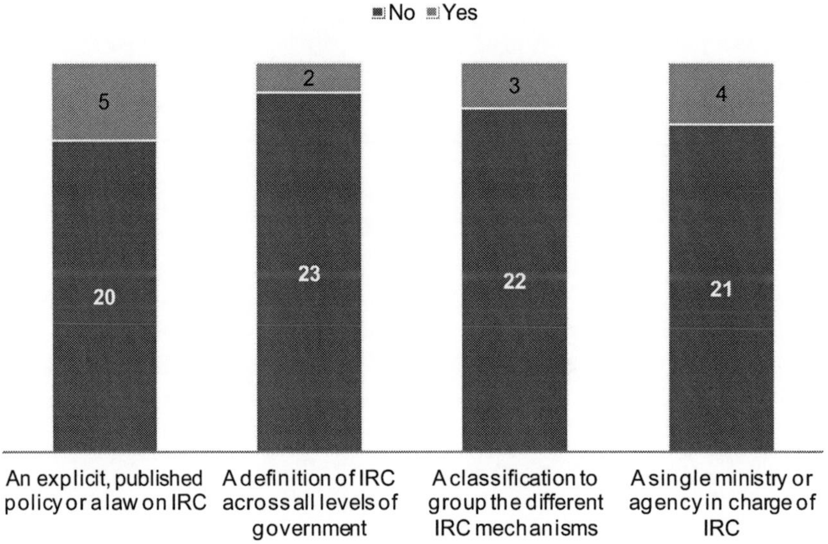

■No ■Yes

| An explicit, published policy or a law on IRC | A definition of IRC across all levels of government | A classification to group the different IRC mechanisms | A single ministry or agency in charge of IRC |

Source: OECD (2012), Survey on International Regulatory Co-operation.

For example, in Sweden, while the Ministry for Foreign Affairs generally handles issues related to IRC, the National Board of Trade participates in various horizontal forums (EU, MAAC, WTO-TBT, UNECE, OECD), and line ministries and national sectoral authorities/government agencies participate within their area of responsibility and competence in sector-specific forums. In New Zealand, a number of line departments take the lead in IRC in their areas of responsibility. The Ministry of Foreign Affairs and Trade is consulted when formal instruments are being negotiated.

The growing role of transnational private regulation

With markets and regulatory tasks are becoming increasingly global, forms of private IRC have emerged and proliferated along with – or sometimes as a replacement for – traditional forms of inter-governmental co-operation. This trend responds to the difficulties in co-ordinating the inconsistencies between standard setting and enforcement, the divergences between administrative and judicial enforcement, and asymmetries of information, which emerge at the transnational level and make purely public regulatory co-operation an insufficient response. In particular, the case study on transnational private regulation identifies four factors that explain the development of international private regulation:

- The production of certain goods and services that transcends national boundaries and does not lend itself easily to direct regulation by national legislation. This is the case with international public goods such as deforestation and emission reduction.

- The extension of global value chains to countries in which the rule of law is not entirely complied with and where contractual governance replaces public domestic institutions.

- The development of markets where the fast pace of change and highly technical information needed to regulate (typically in relation to high-tech and knowledge-intensive activities) lead policymakers to rely on private parties, at least for the definition of technical specifications.

- The importance of private actors' expertise in a number of policy issues, as the most informed parties, the best positioned players to solve a given failure, or the parties in control of essential resources.

Transnational private regulation (TPR) schemes vary enormously in terms of composition, mission, geographic reach, governance structures, and regulatory functions. The most common forms of regulatory output produced by TPR schemes are codes of conduct, guidelines, commercial contract schemes, industry standards and social or environmental standards. According to the case study on transnational private regulation, the two main vehicles for TPR are organisations and contracts. Organisations can have various forms (association, foundation, for profit, not for profit, etc.). Organisations first and foremost regulate the behaviour of their members, but may also impact third parties. Commercial contracts are increasingly being used in addition to the traditional codes of conduct and guidelines, as a means of ensuring compliance throughout supply chains and across state boundaries (Cafaggi, 2012). This last feature reflects the increasing use of supply chains as regulatory vehicles. An example is the leading UK clothing retailer Marks and Spencers that requires suppliers to reduce energy consumption by 10% in its top 100 clothing factories.[8]

The case study on consumer product safety provides an example of TPR in support of public policy making. The GS1 is a non-profit organisation, which develops voluntary standards for businesses and facilitates their co-operation at international level. It has developed a product taxonomy, which is a classification system for grouping products through use of the Global Trade Item Numbers (GTIN). The system is used by businesses, regulators and the OECD Working Party on Consumer Product Safety to develop a Global Portal on Product Recalls. Its use is also being considered by the customs authorities. It is particularly helpful in supply chain management and has also supported market surveillance actions by regulators. For example, thanks to this system, the consumer protection authority in Korea has been able to block unsafe products at the point of sale within half an hour after receiving information that a product poses a risk to consumers.

Initially, as shown in the case study on transnational private regulation, TPR developed as a sector specific regulation, in areas such as the environment, private security services, financial markets, technical standards, e-commerce, etc. More recently, however, consolidation of the various TPR schemes is occurring and meta-private regulators have started to emerge and provide general rules applicable to many sectors. An example is the work of ISEAL Alliance, an international non-profit organisation that codifies best practices for the design and implementation of social and environmental standards initiatives. Ultimately, this development has led to the endorsement of ISEAL's efforts by the FAO, which has now taken the leadership in the definition of a global Sustainability Assessment of Food and Agriculture systems (SAFA). Another illustration of this consolidation trend is provided by the recent "umbrella" standards issued by ISO that are bringing together previous standards under a common framework (such as ISO 2600 Standard on Social Responsibility). This consolidation of co-operative mechanisms is driven by a number of factors (developed in the case study on transnational private regulation, based on Cafaggi, 2011), including the need to address the proliferation of schemes, to avoid conflicts across various schemes, to reduce costs through standardisation, to enhance quality and effectiveness, and to improve enforcement and compliance.

The "simultaneous privatisation and internationalisation of governance", as described in Büthe and Mattli (2012), can be illustrated by the growing delegation of regulatory authority to international private standard-setting bodies. An example of this trend is provided by Figure 1.2, which shows the steady increase in number of ISO standards over the years.

As developed in the case study on transnational private regulation and Büthe and Mattli (2012), technical standard-setting bodies can be public or private. They are large in number, often specialised in a specific area and generally monopolistic in their area of activity. Some of the large, international and long-established bodies include the International Organization for Standardization (ISO, Box 1.10), the International Telecommunications Union (ITU), the International Electronic Commission (IEC), the World Wide Web Consortium (W3C), and the Codex Alimentarius Commission. Another is the IASB (International Accounting

Standards Board), which has produced the International Financial Reporting Standards (IFRS) adopted internationally for the accounting and reporting of corporate financial information. According to Büthe and Mattli (2012), "ISO and IEC jointly account for 85% of all international product standards". ISO, ITU and IEC form the World Standards Cooperation Alliance, a co-operative approach aimed at strengthening the voluntary standard setting regime. In addition, a number of regional technical standard setters provide for harmonised technical standards within a specific region, such as the European Committee for Standardization (CEN), the Pan American Standards Commission (COPANT), and the African Organization for Standardization (ARSO).

The importance of standard-setting bodies has been formalised in the Agreement on Technical Barriers to Trade of 1994, which requires WTO members to use relevant international standards as the basis for their technical regulations when they exist or when their completion is imminent (Article 2.4). Similarly, within the EU, the New Approach introduced in 1985 supported the delegation of regulatory authority to private standardisation bodies for the elaboration of technical specifications. Countries recognise that products manufactured according to the standards set by these organisations conform to the requirements specified in the EU Directives and permit their free circulation. Application of harmonised standards remains "voluntary" in a way that the manufacturer may apply other technical specifications to meet the requirements.[9] However, Büthe and Mattli (2012) highlight the fact that regulations that use international standards are presumed to be consistent with the country's WTO obligations, while the use of a different standard may be challenged through the WTO dispute resolution mechanism as a non-tariff barrier to trade. Consequently, although international technical standards (issued by ISO or CEN for instance) are voluntary, they have *de facto* become largely binding in practice because of their reference in key legal documents – domestic laws and regulations, and trade agreements.

Box 1.10. The development of the International Organization for Standardization (ISO)

Since the establishment of the world's first international private standard-setting organisation, the International Electrotechnical Commission (IEC) in 1906, the number of international product standards has increased immensely (as has the number of standard-setting bodies). IEC's sister organisation, the International Organization for Standardization (ISO), alone has published more than 26 000 International Standards since its founding date in 1946. Today, members from 164 countries develop ISO standards through a consensus process, at the rate of around 1 000 new standards per year in the last decade. While "relatively hidden from public view" (Murphy and Yates, 2009), ISO and IEC have established themselves as "the truly international standard-setters for manufactured goods" (Buthe and Mattli, 2011), and have become undisputed key players in their areas by the Agreement on Technical Barriers to Trade of 1994. As Murphy and Yates (2009) note, ISO has even taken on some of the tasks that have proven too difficult for the League of Nations or the UN, including environmental regulation and corporate responsibility for human rights (e.g. ISO 14000 and ISO 26000).

ISO was established through a merger between the International Federation of National Standardizing Associations (ISA) and the United Nations Standards Coordinating Committee (UNSCC). The organisation is comprised of national standard-setting bodies, the majority of which are private-sector organisations from industrialised countries and largely funded by industry. Together with a variety of actors from industry, academia, society and government they form about 250 technical committees and decide on standards upon a request from business, government or society (although governments are not formally part of the negotiations). All decisions from the technical committees, subcommittees and working groups are concluded by consensus at each stage of the ISO process. However, consensus does not necessarily mean to achieve unanimity but "striving for the greatest feasible agreement among the technical preferences of the member countries that have taken a position on a (draft) standard" (Buthe and Mattli, 2011).

While ISO was mainly concerned with the mechanical field in its early years, it has quickly moved into new areas, such as chemical technology, construction materials, nuclear and solar energy, ergonomics, as well as air and water quality. Together with the consumer movement in industrialised countries in the late 1960s, the ISO has moved away from producing standards covering basic test methods and terminologies towards developing standards related to the design or performance, as well as safety and health aspects, of industrial and consumer products. The expansion of global trade and product market integration in the 1980s led international standards to further move to environmental, health, and safety issues.

The adoption of the Agreement on Technical Barriers to Trade in 1994 led to an immense expansion of standard-setting activity of both the ISO and IEC. The ISO and IEC standards have expanded not only into a wide range of new domains, including information technologies, nanotechnology, biometrics, health care, e-commerce, fisheries, aqua-culture, and quality management (ISO 9000-series), and environmental management (ISO 14 000-series standards) but also across rapidly emerging countries, such as Singapore, Brazil, China and India.

Source: Based on Büthe, T. and W. Mattli (2012), *The New Global Rulers: The Privatization of Regulation in the World Economy*, Princeton University Press, Princeton; and ISO (www.iso.org).

Notes

1. Among the exceptions, US President Barack Obama issued on 1 May 2012 an Executive Order on International Regulatory Cooperation, defining IRC as "referring to a bilateral, regional or multilateral process in which national governments engage in various forms of collaboration and communication with respect to regulations, in particular a process that is reasonably anticipated to lead to the development of significant regulations". www.whitehouse.gov/the-press-office/2012/05/01/executive-order-promoting-international-regulatory-cooperation.

2. At the time of completion of this report, APEC is developing a toolkit on IRC that incorporates a list of options for co-operation.

3. Australia: www.info.dfat.gov.au/info/treaties/treaties.nsf; Estonia: www.riigiteataja.ee; New Zealand: www.mfat.govt.nz/Treaties-and-International-Law/index.php.

4. Overview on trends in regional trade agreements and database of agreements maintained by the WTO: www.wto.org/english/tratop_e/region_e/region_e.htm.

5. The EU provides the example of the MRA with Switzerland, which deals partly with mutual recognition of certificates in areas where Swiss and EU regulations are the same; and the MRA on marine equipment, for which the underlying regulations are International Maritime Organisation Conventions (IMO) agreed by both the United States and the EU Member States.

6. EU submission to the OECD survey on IRC and http://ec.europa.eu/enterprise/policies/single-market-goods/international-aspects/mutual-recognition-agreement/index_en.htm.

7. The OECD Council Decision adopted in 1981 concerning the Mutual Acceptance of Data in the Assessment of Chemicals states that data generated in a Member country in accordance with OECD Test Guidelines and Principles of Good Laboratory Practice (GLP) shall be accepted in other Member countries for assessment purposes and other uses relating to the protection of human health and the environment. The Council Decision-Recommendation on Compliance with GLP adopted in

1989 provides safeguards for assurance that the data is indeed developed in compliance with the Principles of GLP. It establishes procedures for monitoring GLP compliance through government inspections and study audits as well as a framework for international liaison among monitoring and data-receiving authorities. Governments agree to recognise the results of inspections by compliance monitoring programmes conducted in other OECD countries and MAD adherents.

8.   See OECD (2010a) for the description of various private and public-private partnerships to mitigate GHG emissions in supply chains.

9.   EC Guide to the implementation of directives based on the New Approach and the Global Approach: http://ec.europa.eu/enterprise/policies/single-market-goods/files/blue-guide/guidepublic_en.pdf.

Bibliography

Abbott, K. and D. Snidal (2010), "International Regulation without International Government: Improving IO Performance through Orchestration", Vol. 5, *Review of International Organizations*, p. 315.

Abbott, K. and D. Snidal (2009), "Strengthening International Regulation Trough Transnational New Governance: Overcoming the Orchestration Deficit", *Vanderbilt Journal of Transnational Law*, Vol. 42, pp. 501-578.

Abbott, K. and D. Snidal (2000), "Hard and Soft Law in International Governance", *International Organization,* Vol. 54, No. 3, pp. 421-456.

Alvarez, J. (2005), *International Organizations as Law-Makers*, Oxford University Press, New York.

Australia and New Zealand Productivity Commissions (2012), "Strengthening trans-Tasman Economic Relations", Discussion Draft, September.

Boyer, R. and D. Drache (eds) (1996), *The Power of Markets and the Future of the Nation State,* Routledge, London.

Braithwaite, J. and P. Drahos (eds.) (2000), *Global Business Regulation*, Cambridge University Press, Cambridge.

Büthe, T. and W. Mattli (2012), *The New Global Rulers: The Privatization of Regulation in the World Economy*, Princeton University Press, Princeton.

Cafaggi F. (2012), "The Regulatory Function of Transnational Commercial Contracts: New architectures", European University Institute - Department of Law (LAW).

Cafaggi F. (2011), "New Foundations of Transnational Private Regulation", *Journal of Law and Society.*

Commission of the European Communities (1985), Completing the Internal Market, White Paper from the Commission to the European Council, (COM(85)310 final).

Drezner, D. (2007), *All Politics is Global,* Princeton University Press, Princeton.

Esty D.C. and D. Geradin (2000), "Regulatory Co-opetition", *Journal of International Economic Law*, Vol. 3, Issue 2, pp. 235-255, Oxford.

EU (1985), Council Resolution on a new approach to technical harmonisation and standards.

Falk, R. (1997), "State of Siege: Will Globalization Win Out?", *International Affairs*, 73, pp. 123-36.

Farber, D. (2011), "Legal guidelines for cooperation between the EU and American state governments", in: D. Vogel and J. Swinnen (eds.), *Transatlantic Regulatory Cooperation,* Edward Elgar, Northhampton.

Fliess, B. et al. (2010), "The Use of International Standards in Technical Regulation", *OECD Trade Policy Working Papers*, No. 102, OECD Publishing, Paris.

Hioureas C. and B. Cain (2010), *Transatlantic Environmental Regulation-Making: Strengthening Cooperation between California and the European Union*, Edward Elgar Publications.

Industry Canada (2002), "International Regulatory Co-operation", quoted in Policy Research Initiative.

Kahler, M. and D. Lake (2011), "Economic Integration and Global Governance: Why So Little Supranationalism?", in W. Mattli and N. Woods (eds.), *The Politics of Global Regulation*, Princeton University Press.

Keohane R. and J. Nye (1974), "Transgovernmental Relations and the International Organisations", *World Politics*, Vol. 26, Issue 1, pp. 39-62.

Koenig-Archibugi, M. (2010), "Global Regulation", in: R. Baldwin et al. (eds.), *The Oxford Handbook of Regulation,* Oxford University Press, Oxford.

Levy B. (2011), "Innovations in Globalised Regulation", *Policy Research Working Paper*, World Bank.

Majone, G. (1996), "Regulating Europe", *European Public Policy Services*, J. Richardson (ed.), Routledge, New York.

Majone, G. (1994), "The Rise of the Regulatory State in Europe", *West European Politics*, Vol. 17, pp. 77-101.

Mattli, W. and N. Woods (eds.) (2009), *The Politics of Global Regulation*, Princeton University Press.

Mattli, W. and T. Buthe (2003), "Setting International Standards: Technological Rationality or Primacy of Power?", *World Politics,* 56(1), pp. 1–42.

Meuwese A. (2009), "EU-U.S. Horizontal Regulatory Cooperation", Paper for the California-EU Regulatory Cooperation Project Leuven, Conference Brussels, 10 June.

Mugge, D. (2006), "Private-Public Puzzles: Inter-firm Competition and Transnational Private Regulation", *New Political Economy*, Vol. 11 (2), pp. 177-200.

Murphy, C. and J. Yates (2009), *The International Organization for Standardization (ISO). Global Governance through voluntary consensus*, Routledge, New York.

Nicolaidis, K. and G. Shaffer (2005), "Managed Mutual Recognition Regimes: Governance Without Global Government", *Law and Contemporary Problems*, Vol. 68, pp. 263-318; University of Wisconsin Legal Studies Research Paper No. 1007; IILJ Working Paper No. 2005/6.

OECD (2012a), *Recommendation of the Council on Regulatory Policy and Governance*, OECD, Paris.

OECD (2010a), *Transition to a Low-Carbon Economy: Public Goals and Corporate Practices*, OECD Publishing. doi: 10.1787/9789264090231-en.

OECD (2010b), *Cutting Costs in Chemicals Management: How OECD Helps Governments and Industry*, OECD Publishing. doi: 10.1787/9789264085930-en.

OECD (1998), "Regulatory Reform and International Standardisation", Paris.

OECD (1994), *Regulatory Cooperation for an Interdependent World*, OECD Publishing, Paris.

Raustiala, K. (2002), "The Architecture of International Cooperation: Transgovernmental · Networks and the Future of International Law", *Virginia Journal of International Law Association*, Vol. 43, Issue 1.

Schmidt, S. (2012), "Transnational governance through mutual recognition", paper prepared for the Conference on the distributional effects of transnational regulation, Rome, May.

Slaugther, A. (1997), "The Real New World Order", *Foreign Affairs*, Vol. 76, Issue 5, New York, pp. 183-197.

Steger, D. (2012), "Institutions for Regulatory Cooperation in 'New Generation' Economic and Trade Agreements", *Legal Issues of Economic Integration*, Vol. 38, No. 4, pp. 109-126.

Stewart R. (2012), "The enforcement of transnational regulation", in F. Cafaggi (ed.), *The enforcement of transnational regulation.*

Strange, S. (1996), *The Retreat of the State: The Diffusion of Power in the World Economy,* Cambridge University Press.

The Australia and New Zealand School of Government (n.d.), Arrangements for facilitating trans-Tasman government institutional co-operation, Australia Department of Finance and Administration and New Zealand Ministry of Economic Development.

Urpelainen, J. (2009), "All or Nothing: Avoiding Inefficient Compromise in International Cooperation", Dissertation at the University of Michigan.

Verdier, H. (2009), "Transnational Regulatory Networks and Their Limits", *The Yale Journal of International Law*, Vol. 34, pp. 113-172.

Vogel, D. and J. Swinnen (eds.) (2011), *Transatlantic Regulatory Cooperation: The Shifting Roles of the EU, the US and California,* Edward Elgar, Northhampton.

Wolf, A. and J. Hammer (2000), "Trends in Transboundary Water Disputes and Dispute Resolution", in: *Environment and Security* (ed. by Lowi, Miriam R. and Brian R. Shaw), London: MacMillan Press Ltd; New York: St. Martins's Press, Inc, pp. 123-148.

World Trade Organisation (2012), *World Trade Report 2012, Trade and Public Policies: A Closer Look at Non-tariff Measures in the 21st Century.*

Chapter 2

Building successful international regulatory co-operation

Despite the growing trend in regulatory co-operation, decision making on IRC is not based on a clear understanding of benefits, costs and success factors of the various IRC options. This chapter is a preliminary attempt to define the range of benefits and costs/challenges of IRC. It identifies quantitative evidence of benefits and costs available to date and complements it with lessons learnt from the OECD IRC case studies. This chapter also builds on the case studies and the literature to identify some of the success factors of IRC and to initiate a checklist of critical considerations for government to ensure successful IRC.

In a context where countries are increasingly entering into a wide variety of co-operative arrangements to keep pace with the need to regulate across borders, a thorough understanding of the benefits, costs and success factors of IRC is needed. To date, however, most cases of successful co-operation within the OECD have developed in an ad hoc manner, along paths of least resistance, often without a clear understanding of the results to be expected. Achievements have been made in fairly specific and limited areas. Uncertainty about the benefits and costs of regulatory co-operation and the absence of a theoretical framework to systematise and rationalise decision making on regulatory co-operation help explain the ad hoc character of some IRC experiences. Such uncertainty may also increase the likelihood that IRC discussions are driven by ideology rather than by an evidence-based approach.

Ultimately, there is a need to develop a theoretical framework that can systematise and rationalise decision making on regulatory co-operation and help monitor its outcomes – based on an assessment component evaluating the benefits, costs and effectiveness of various alternative IRC mechanisms in specific contexts and a checklist of key considerations for developing beneficial co-operation. This chapter lays the foundation for such guidance by gathering evidence on the benefits, costs and challenges of IRC, and on the success factors and critical elements of co-operation.

Understanding the costs and benefits of IRC

The literature and available evidence point towards a number of generic benefits and challenges associated with IRC. For the purpose of this report, they have been grouped in four categories that reflect the literature and available evidence (see Figure 2.1). The benefits encompass the economic gains from reduced costs on economic activity and increased trade and investment flows, the progress in managing risks and externalities across borders, administrative efficiency from greater transparency and work-sharing across governments and public authorities, as well as knowledge flow and peer learning. The challenges include the co-ordination costs, sovereignty issues and the lack of regulatory flexibility, the difficult political economy of regulatory co-operation, and implementation bottlenecks.

Whether the benefits outweigh the challenges and costs in specific instances will depend on various elements, including the sector under consideration, the characteristics of the countries involved in the partnership, and the process by which co-operation is developed. But while the literature and case studies generally support the view that regulatory co-operation carries important benefits, the quantitative evidence on the benefits and costs of IRC remains limited. This section first reviews the limited quantitative evidence available on the benefits and costs of IRC and then turns to define them building on a review of the literature, the lessons learnt from the IRC case studies, and country perceptions from the IRC Survey.

Figure 2.1. Schematic approach to benefits, costs and challenges of IRC

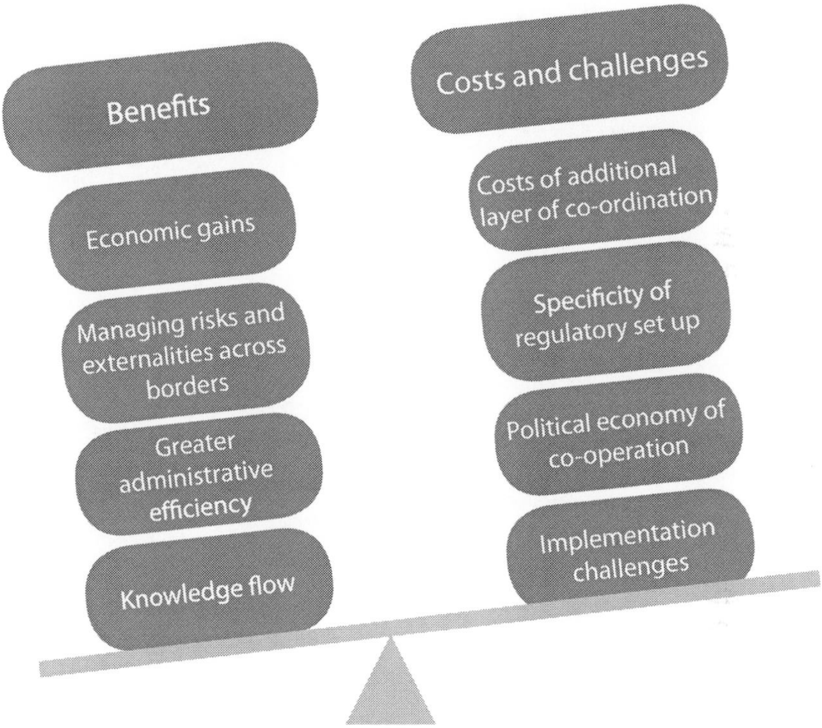

Benefits

Costs and challenges

Economic gains

Costs of additional layer of co-ordination

Managing risks and externalities across borders

Specificity of regulatory set up

Greater administrative efficiency

Political economy of co-operation

Knowledge flow

Implementation challenges

Source: OECD elaboration, 2012.

The paucity of quantitative evidence on benefits, challenges and costs

Some efforts have been made in the past to estimate the broad/macroeconomic benefits of regulatory alignment, in particular in terms of trade and FDI gains, increased competitiveness and productivity, and higher income (see Table 2.1 for a summary). However, these estimates show important weaknesses in relation to their broad nature. In particular, they cannot be used to identify concretely which measures would yield the greatest benefits. They cannot help either to differentiate regulatory burden at federal, provincial or municipal levels.

Table 2.1. Estimates of aggregate economic benefits from regulatory co-operation

Estimated magnitude of the benefits	Source / methodology
Trade gains	
Regulatory co-operation that decreases (Canadian or American) domestic regulatory burden by 10% could yield an increase of 2.5% in exports of goods and services.	Policy Research Initiative (2004) based on OECD estimates of various elasticities.
If regulatory co-operation reduced regulatory burdens to the level of the world leader (the United Kingdom), Canada and the United States could expect gains of 32% and 14% respectively in exports of goods, and 44% and 20% respectively in exports of services.	
A 10% decrease in a country's FDI restrictions could increase its exports of goods and services by 0.4% and 1.3%, respectively.	
Testing and inspection procedures by importers in developed countries are found to reduce exports of developing countries by 9% and 3%, respectively. Diverging standards reduce the likelihood of exporting to more than three markets by 7%.	Chen, M.X., T. Otsuki, J.S. Wilson (2006), using the World Bank Technical Barriers to Trade Survey database
In the United States, harmonisation of data through the use of global trade item numbers (GTINs) could reduce the volume of consumer toy products subject to examination by the US Consumer Product Safety Commission by 75%, the equivalent of USD 16.8 million in savings for toy importers and USD 775 000 in savings for CPSC over 5 years.	Case study on consumer product safety (2012).
Standards and related technical regulations that differ inhibit efficient mass production (economies of scale) and increase the cost of foreign goods – equivalent to a tariff of 2 to 10%.	Kawamoto et al. (1997).
Potential trade facilitation measures for ports, customs, regulation, and service sector infrastructure could lead to global increases in merchandise trade of USD 377 billion, i.e. about a 9.7% increase in total trade.	Wilson and C. Mann (2005).
Increased (Foreign Direct Investment) FDI	
If Canada had had the same degree of regulatory restrictiveness as the United States from 1976 to 1998, investments would have on average increased by approximately USD 1 billion per year.	Policy Research Initiative (2004).
If Canada's regulatory regime had changed at the same pace as that of the United States', total investment in the Canadian economy would have been higher by about USD 400 million per year, on average. In other words, Canada could have had an average of 30% more investment per year than what it actually had over the period.	
Increased innovation, competitiveness and productivity	
The EU Single Market Programme was found to be associated with an R&D intensity that was 7.3 percentage points higher than in its absence.	Griffith, Harrison, and Simpson (2006).
In addition, a one percentage point increase in R&D intensity is associated with a 0.6 percentage point increase in total factor productivity (TFP) growth.	

Table 2.1. Estimates of aggregate economic benefits
from regulatory co-operation (*cont.*)

Estimated magnitude of the benefits	Source / methodology
Higher income and employment	
Convergence between Canadian and American regulatory burdens would increase per capita income in Canada by up to 2%.	Policy Research Initiative (2004).
EU-wide GDP and the EU level of employment would have been 1.8% and 1.5% lower in the absence of the Single Market Programme.	Dierx and Schmidt (2005)
Eliminating half of the non-tariff barriers to trade caused by regulatory divergences could increase EU GDP by 0.7% in 2018 compared to the baseline scenario (do nothing) representing an annual potential gain of EUR 122 billion. The same operation would yield a 0.3% gain in the US GDP, representing an annual potential gain of EUR 41 billion.	ECORYS (2009)
A combination of elimination of tariffs and of non-tariff measures would increase economic welfare by EUR 33 billion in the EU and by EUR 18 billion in Japan. A third of the benefits for the EU would come from tariff dismantling, the rest from NTM reduction. For Japan, the vast majority of benefits would be generated by NTM reduction. The export effects stemming from a reduction of NTMs alone would amount to EUR 29 billion for the EU and to EUR 28 billion for Japan.	Copenhagen Economics (2009)
OECD (2011) analyses the economic consequences of more liberal tariff and NTM regimes (notably changes in real GDP, employment, exports and national income) for individual G20 countries and regional groupings. For example, a 50% reduction in NTMs would lead to a GDP gains for the Euro Zone of 1.8% (short run) / 6.6% (long run), for the US of 0.9% (short run) / 3.5% (long run), for the UK of 1.5% (short run) / 4.8% (long run), and for Australia of 0.6% (short run) / 5% (long run).	OECD (2011). Based on a general equilibrium model.
The welfare effects of removal of selected NTBs lead to global gains of USD 90 billion, arising mostly from liberalisation in Japan and Europe and in the textile and machinery sectors.	Andriamanajara et al. (2004). Based on a general equilibrium model.
OECD governments and industry save approximately EUR 153 million per year, through reduced chemical testing (due to the MAD system) as well as the harmonisation of chemical safety tools and policies across jurisdictions.	OECD (2010a).

Source: Based on an input provided by the Canada RCC Secretariat and various references mentioned in the second column.

The paucity of quantitative approaches can be explained by the difficulty in gathering detailed information on the impact of regulatory divergences. For example, in Canada, there are approximately 2 600 federal regulations in place covering 14 sectors. In the United States, federal agencies published 132 820 final rules in the Federal Register between 1981 and 2009. Analysing each Canadian and United States regulation in order to identify misalignments and assess their economic impact would require significant resources. An additional difficulty relates to the fact that regulatory misalignment is not necessarily the product of differing regulations, but often results from different applications of regulations, including independent approvals of the same products, different nomenclature of products, re-inspection of products at the border, additional certification or administrative requirements, and different testing procedures.

The difficulty of undertaking quantitative analysis of the benefits of regulatory co-operation or of the costs associated with a lack of regulatory co-operation in specific sectors has been flagged as a critical impediment to the development of regulatory partnerships in the case study on the Regulatory Cooperation Council (RCC) between Canada and the United States. In the case of the RCC, evidence on benefits is mainly qualitative or anecdotal. The imprecision of this type of information makes it difficult to communicate the precise benefits of this initiative to the public. Consequently, going forward, the RCC Secretariat in Canada will devote efforts to improving both micro- and macroeconomic analysis to fill this gap, most notably through sector-based case studies. The sectoral approach has been identified as the most likely to provide meaningful benefits and cost estimates. In addition, rather than adopting a systematic review of current regulations, the RCC will focus its efforts on the development of alignment mechanisms between Canadian and US regulators to ensure that future opportunities for regulatory alignment are maximised to pre-empt the development of unnecessary diverging regulatory practices.

The OECD IRC Survey shows the absence of systematic approaches to costs and benefits of IRC at a country level: no country reports undertaking a systematic cost-benefit analysis of its IRC initiatives. In a number of countries, however, treaty ratification deserves a specific attention. In both Australia and New Zealand, for instance, treaties are tabled in the Parliament with a National Interest Analysis (NIA), which notes the reasons why the country should become a party to the treaty (see Box 2.1).

Box 2.1. **National Interest Analysis (NIA)**

In **New Zealand,** Standing Order 389 requests that the NIA be prepared by the government departments managing the treaty for every multilateral treaty and for "major bilateral treaties of particular significance" to New Zealand. The NIA should outline:

- Date of proposed binding treaty action;

- Reasons for New Zealand to become Party to the treaty;

- Advantages and disadvantages to New Zealand of the treaty entering into force;

- Obligations that would be imposed on New Zealand by the treaty action;

- Measures the Government could or should adopt to implement the treaty;

- Economic, social, cultural and environmental effects – must include consideration of potential impact on Māori interests;

- Costs to New Zealand of compliance with the treaty;

- Future protocols or amendments to the treaty;

- Consultation; and

- Withdrawal or denunciation provision in the treaty.

In **Australia,** the NIA includes a discussion of the foreseeable economic, environmental, social and cultural effects of the treaty action; the obligations imposed by the treaty; its direct financial costs to Australia; how the treaty will be implemented domestically; what consultation has occurred in relation to the treaty action and whether the treaty provides for withdrawal or denunciation. Treaties which affect business or restrict competition are also required to be tabled with a Regulation Impact Statement (RIS).

Source: Based on answers to the OECD IRC Survey and country several websites: Australian Treaties Library: www.austlii.edu.au/au/other/dfat; New Zealand: www.mfat.govt.nz/Treaties-and-International-Law/03-Treaty-making-process/2-National-Interest-Analyses/index.php and http://cabguide.cabinetoffice.govt.nz/procedures/international-treaty-making/national-interest-analysis.

In addition, there are examples of the use of RIAs at supranational or inter-governmental level. A key example is the use of RIA for EU regulation. Another one is the requirement in New Zealand and Australia that decision-making by Ministerial Councils in relation to Trans-Tasman Mutual Recognition Agreement (TTMRA) matters be informed by the COAG 'Principles and Guidelines for National Standard Setting and Regulatory Action'. Regulatory Impact Statements (RIS) that fall within the ambit of the TTMRA are reviewed by both the Australian Office of Best

Practice Regulation and New Zealand RIA Unit. Despite these examples, the evidence rather points towards the fact that while IGOs and other international organisations (international standard setting bodies) play a growing role in supporting regulatory co-operation in multiple areas, they rarely do so based on good regulatory policy governance and tools, such as RIAs, to support their rule making processes.

Sector level information on benefits and costs seems to be underdeveloped as well. Control of chemicals provides an isolated case where systematic efforts have been undertaken to assess the benefits and costs of IRC (as illustrated in the case study on chemical safety). In 2010, the OECD conducted an analysis to determine the savings that governments and industry accrue from their participation in the OECD EHS Programme, focusing on the benefits of harmonisation (e.g., through the MAD system) and burden sharing (e.g., from working together through the HPV programme). Consequently, annual net savings resulting from the OECD's EHS Programme were estimated at EUR 153 million.

It is not likely that the costs of the infrastructure running the co-operation itself – in the cases of relatively "light" institutional co-operative agreements – constitutes a primary challenge to the success of IRC. As an example, the cost of maintaining the consumer product safety platform is estimated at between EUR 215 000 to EUR 340 000 per year. The costs of the EHS Programme (OECD Secretariat costs and country costs) were estimated to reach EUR 15 million in 2010 (OECD, 2010b). Similarly, the costs of administering the Canada/US RCC are considered to be limited. The majority of staff in the Canadian secretariat of the RCC are seconded from their home departments for the duration of this initiative. The only administrative costs relate to the implementation of the various initiatives within the regulatory departments and agencies – e.g., dedicated person time, travel, etc. However, as illustrated in the next section, in the long run, the need for continuous financial support may become a challenge for the continuity of co-operation, especially in the context of budget constraints.

While it is not always easy to estimate the direct benefits of co-operation, in a few instances the case studies have highlighted the importance of the costs of inaction (i.e. of not co-operating). In the product safety area, for instance, increased co-operation would contribute to reducing the number of injuries through the removal of dangerous products from markets in a timelier manner. Ultimately, this would help address treatment costs estimated to exceed USD 1 trillion per year. Similarly, according to OECD (1994), eliminating the "costs of non-Europe" through the removal of obstacles and inconsistency attributable to administrative burdens and non-tariff barriers created by the existing 12 regulatory regimes was a key element of the case for the completion of the EC internal market.

The cost of inaction, which has been politically influential in some areas, may nonetheless be difficult to carry out in other areas. The case study on chemical safety highlights this difficulty and attributes it to the complexity of quantifying the effects of chemicals on human health and the environment, as well as the impacts that chemical safety policies have on avoiding such effects. The case study nevertheless provides estimates from an administrative point of view, of the cost for a pesticide company to test for health and environmental effects (around EUR 17 million). When health and environmental requirements are not aligned, this cost is multiplied by the number of different requests. Similarly, resources needed for a government to review and assess the data are around 2.2 person / year – multiplied by the number of countries where assessment is needed.

While the quantitative estimates of benefits from IRC are scarce, the case studies show that the intangible and qualitative elements are likely to represent an important part of the expected benefits of IRC. They are even likely to be as important as the quantified benefits. In the case of co-operation in the chemical area, such benefits include the health and environmental gains from governments being able to evaluate and manage more chemicals than they would if working independently; or the development of new and more effective methods for assessing chemicals through countries putting their efforts together. A summary of the non-quantitative benefits of the OECD EHS programme is provided in the case study on chemical safety. The next sections build on the IRC case studies and the literature survey to define and classify the benefits, costs and challenges of IRC.

The benefits of IRC

Overall, the case studies and the OECD IRC survey confirm the potential benefits from IRC highlighted in the literature, which this report has grouped into four categories: economic gains, progress in managing risks and externalities across borders; administrative efficiency; and knowledge flow. Table 2.4 summarises the findings on IRC benefits from the IRC case studies. Figure 2.2 illustrates the answers given by countries to the question: "Based on your past experiences of regulatory co-operation, please indicate the importance of the following potential benefits of international regulatory co-operation for your country".[1]

Economic gains

The literature generally supports the view that regulatory co-operation leads to economic gains through reduced transaction costs and economies of scale. Regulatory convergence is expected to permit firms to "utilize standardized contracts, documents and procedures to achieve economies of scale, reduce search and transaction costs, and simplify bargaining" (Lazer, 2001). Identical regulations should help reduce the cost of production by allowing companies to maintain single production processes, rather than multiple processes to accommodate for multiple standards regimes (Drezner, 2007). Similarly, Ahearn (CRS Report for US Congress, 2009) emphasises the impact of policy co-ordination on transaction costs. Abbott and Snidal (2000) suggests that the decrease in marginal costs for firms resulting from increased regulatory co-operation will in turn generate an increase in consumer surplus and social welfare (e.g. through greater product choice, lower prices, faster access to new products). Similarly, increased information sharing allowed by greater co-operation should lead to a decrease in domestic funds spent on duplicative scientific and policy research, freeing resources that in turn could be allocated to more efficient uses.

Figure 2.2. Importance of potential benefits of international regulatory co-operation

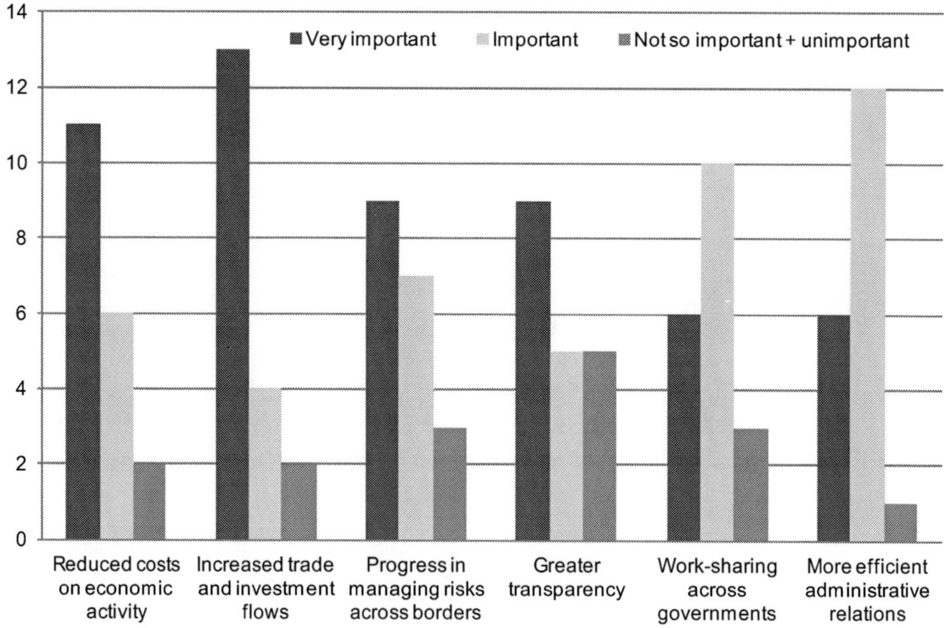

Source: OECD (2012), Survey on International Regulatory Co-operation.

Regulatory co-operation can improve market access and increase trade and investment flows. As noted by Drezner (2007), "uncoordinated, disparate regulatory structures function as implicit barriers to trade". The literature that investigates the effects of regulatory barriers on trade, assimilated to non-tariff measures (NTM) or technical barriers to trade (TBT), is vast and supports the view that, generally, NTMs create at least the same, possibly even greater impediments to trade than tariffs (see OECD, 2011). Since NTMs are not easily detected, it has been difficult for countries to raise disputes in relation to NTM in trade forums, including the WTO. This has supported the approach that NTMs were generally best dealt with through increased co-operation on technical regulations and standards. Along this line, Pettriccione (2000) states that regulatory co-operation "offers the greatest long-term rewards to prevent technical regulations and standards from creating unnecessary trade barriers".

According to the results of the OECD IRC survey (reflected in Figure 2.2), and keeping in mind the caveats related to perception surveys, the most important benefits that countries expect from IRC are the economic gains arising from increased trade and investment flows, and reduced costs on economic activity. Some of the case studies undertaken in support of this work provide a good illustration of the economic gains that can be associated with IRC – typically the case studies on chemical safety, consumer product safety, and the OECD Model Tax Convention (see Table 2.4).

Progress in managing risks and externalities across borders

Intensification of global non-economic challenges, such as those pertaining to the environment (air or water pollution for example), human health or safety, has led to growing efforts at regulatory co-operation across borders. As underlined by Levy (2011), the failure of the market to respond to these challenges traditionally calls for regulatory action. Where externalities are of a global nature, regulators will not be able to address them from a pure domestic angle. Typically, the ability to adequately regulate industrial pollution, trade in hazardous chemicals, infectious diseases, climate change and effectively manage cross-border risks will require co-ordination across neighbouring countries to ensure effectiveness of regulatory measures. If not, the regulatory measures risk being misdirected, inefficient or not adapted.

Without even mentioning the management of global goods, in today's global world, policies adopted in one jurisdiction are likely to have strong extra-territorial implications, to the extent that it may become almost impossible for certain national policy objectives to be achieved without careful consideration of the international context. According to Esty and

Geradin (2000), if regulators ignore impacts beyond their own jurisdiction the standards they set will be systematically suboptimal (too low if they overlook transboundary regulatory benefits and too high if they disregard transboundary regulatory costs). This may prompt regulators to co-operate in order to achieve national regulatory objectives that are strongly affected by freer movement of goods, services and people. In addition, regulatory co-operation may enhance compliance and reduce the risks of a race to the bottom, overall amplifying the impact of domestic regulation.

According to the OECD IRC Survey (Figure 2.2), progress in managing risks across borders comes just after economic gains in terms of perceived benefits by countries. The case studies on energy regulation, transboundary water management and banking supervision illustrate particularly well the importance of IRC to manage global goods and risks (Table 2.4).

Greater administrative efficiency

According to OECD (1994), administrative advantages may be gained through regulatory co-operation. Regulatory co-operation "may exploit the commonality of issues facing regulators at all levels of government, reduce the "learning curve" with respect to new or emerging concerns, increase the speed and effectiveness of regulatory action on cross-border issues, and permit efficient use of scarce information and analytical resources". Work-sharing across governments and public authorities, in which countries co-operate to address similar problems, including at bilateral, regional and multilateral levels may lead to important cost savings that allow countries to rationalise the context of their own regulatory programmes and reallocate scarce public resources to areas of higher priority. Greater transparency may also provide opportunities for more efficient administrative relations with other countries, for instance, through simplification and harmonisation of administrative procedures. The gains may be specific and measurable, or they may be achieved less directly, for instance, through better understanding of the complex interplay between multiple policy goals, which may facilitate national decision-making and policy co-ordination.

All IRC case studies underline the administrative gains and greater transparency that can be achieved through IRC (Table 2.4). According to the OECD IRC survey (Figure 2.2), the administrative gains of IRC are also deemed important by countries – six respondents (one-third of the total) value work-sharing across governments and more efficient administrative relations as very important benefits of IRC. However, compared to economic gains and managing risks across borders, administrative benefits come last and appear rather as collateral gains. This may point to the fact that these benefits may be underestimated by OECD countries (or counterbalanced by other perceived administrative costs).

Knowledge flow and peer learning

Transferring good regulatory practices is an important dimension highlighted across all IRC case studies. In particular, the studies on chemical safety, consumer product safety and prudential regulation of banks mention IRC as an important mechanism to exchange information on regulatory practices between countries with different policy experience and facilitating the access to good practices, making it a capacity building tool. This result reflects the findings in the literature. Meuwese (2009) for instance finds a convergence on norms of standard-setting and regulatory impact assessment through enhanced dialogue between the EU Commission and the US Office of Management and Budget. The horizontal dialogue has both learning (exchange of best practices) and facilitative (reducing trade obstacles and improve sector-specific regulation) aspects. Similarly, according to Raustiala (2002), transgovernmental networks allow "regulatory export", i.e. the export of regulatory rules and practices, which promotes regulatory convergence across states through "network effects". This effect can help build bureaucratic capacity in weaker states, which, in turn, can improve domestic regulation and support regulatory co-operation.

Other potential benefits

The IRC case studies allow going beyond the usual template of economic and administrative benefits of IRC to identify important societal benefits from IRC. The case study on consumer product safety highlights the role of IRC in supporting research on product safety issues. The case study on the OECD Model Tax Convention underlines the importance of uniform interpretation of tax treaties to reduce the potential conflicts between tax payers and tax authorities. The case study on common EU Energy Regulation is seen as having promoted solidarity across countries, security and sustainability of energy supply. Adequate co-operation on transboundary water issues (see case study on transboundary water management) is considered as ultimately fostering food security and poverty alleviation.

The costs and challenges of IRC

Despite the benefits that can be expected, as already highlighted in OECD (1994), IRC remains uneven and non-systematic. Beyond the legitimate concerns of countries that regulatory co-operation may generate costs that outweigh the benefits and of tailoring IRC to their specific needs, the political economy of achieving IRC is seen as complex and the enforcement and implementation of co-operative agreements raise significant challenges.

In a similar way that countries' perception of the benefits from IRC has been in the OECD IRC survey, the survey has tried to capture countries' perception of the challenges associated with IRC through the following question: "Based on your past experiences of regulatory co-operation, please indicate the importance of the following potential concerns raised by engaging in international regulatory co-operation". Figure 2.3 illustrates the answers received in response to this question. It is noteworthy that challenges appear to be less consensual than benefits with countries ranking that the challenge under consideration as not so important, while at the same time others deem it "very important". Also, fewer countries (16) were willing to answer the question about concerns, compared to the question on benefits (19 countries). Table 2.5 summarises the lessons learnt on costs and challenges from the IRC case studies.

Figure 2.3. Importance of potential concerns related to international regulatory co-operation

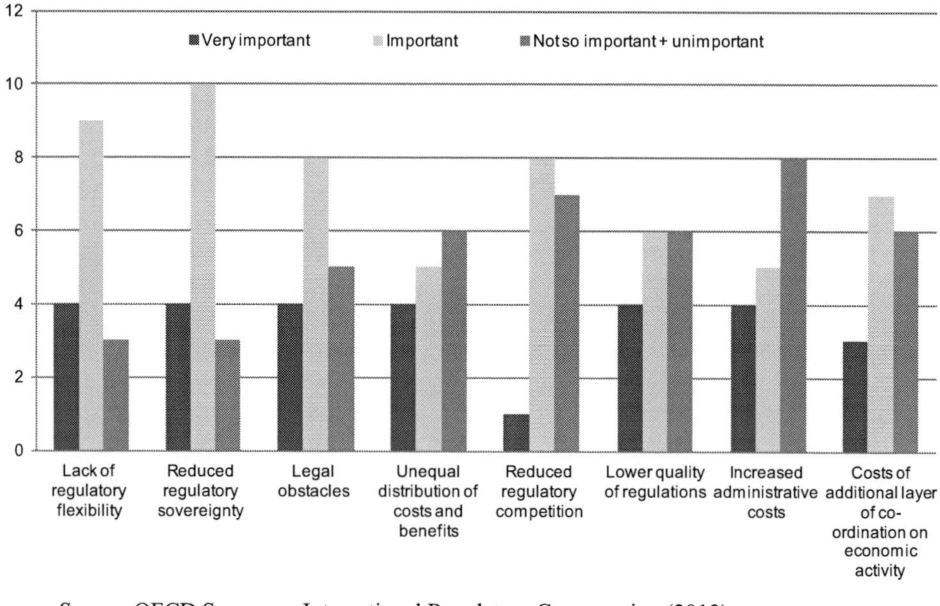

Source: OECD Survey on International Regulatory Co-operation (2012).

Costs

Costs involve the direct costs of the co-ordination infrastructure, i.e. of the IGO, of the secretariat established to manage treaties, of the institution managing the network and of the co-ordinated action. In addition, Drezner (2007) lists a number of direct and indirect costs related to any change in the domestic status quo that co-operation with other jurisdictions may require. The costs for the governments include the time and resources that must be invested in the necessary political capital to make legal and administrative reforms happen, to mobilise bureaucratic actors, to lobby legislatures, and to mollify interest groups. The indirect costs relate to private actors having to retool their operations in order to comply with new regulations.

Sovereignty

According to the OECD IRC Survey, reduced regulatory sovereignty comes first in the concerns of countries with regard to IRC (followed by lack of regulatory flexibility, legal obstacles and lower quality of regulation). Significant hurdles often arise in cases where regulatory co-operation is seen as compromising the principle of regulatory sovereignty or as insufficiently tailored to the needs of a given State or region. Even the application of usually non-controversial procedures can in some cases become sensitive, if they are interpreted as compromising key national interests or values.

A number of scholars focus on the impact of delegation of regulatory powers on accountability. According to Lazer (2001), "since regulatory barriers are increasingly important and the demand to conform to the pressures of the international system can be overwhelming, these processes can result in fundamental accountability problems. That is, potentially, regulatory policies are becoming increasingly detached from the policy preferences of the regulated". Howse (2004) highlights inherent issues of democratic deficits arising from a delegation of powers, which takes place when co-operative regulatory activity is authorised by constitutional representative institutions. Making regulatory co-operation more transparent would help solve this dilemma. However, this may come at the price of reduced effectiveness of regulatory co-operation because the common advantage of informal give-and-take in a climate of trust would be restricted.

In practice, the debate on national preferences and the preservation of sovereignty has been a lively one in Canada according to the Policy Research Initiative (2004). Based on the experience of the regulatory co-operation between Canada and the United States, the Policy Research Initiative mentioned then that "Many Canadians feel strongly about issues affecting their regulatory programs". In particular, people were worried that regulatory co-operation may limit sovereignty and were concerned with preserving Canadian values and identity, to which regulatory diversity contributes – positions that, in the case of the United States and Canada, PRI shows may be more emotional than real because "the differences between Canadian and US values may be more technical than substantial".

At the same time, in a number of IRC experiences, some loss of sovereignty and/or sharing of competences is perceived as being balanced by a stronger international position. Both the Nordic Cooperation and the Australia-New Zealand co-operation highlight the increased influence over policy directions, norms, rules and standards facilitated by a common *ex ante* position among countries.[2] Similarly, the Benelux Union is seen as allowing common contributions from Belgium, Luxembourg and the Netherlands in the EU instances, which give more weight to the position of the three countries.

Regulatory specificity and lack of flexibility

Differences between countries in their regulatory procedures and/or legal systems or traditions may significantly complicate efforts to overcome regulatory divergence. In some cases, regulatory paths are already deeply entrenched making rapprochement difficult. If not insurmountable, lack of regulatory flexibility is mentioned in several case studies as a substantial impediment to IRC. This can take several forms, ranging from differences in approaches to key regulatory concepts and issues, to variations in institutional set up that make the relationships unbalanced. The case study on competition law enforcement provides an example where differences in how competition authorities or courts define confidential information in cartel cases may prevent co-operation. Indeed, since international co-operation instruments usually do not allow for the exchange of confidential information, the competition authorities must demonstrate that the information is not confidential before they are allowed to share it (or put in place specific mechanisms allowing for the exchange of confidential information). If in doubt, the risk of litigation may discourage authorities from disclosing such information to foreign authorities, preventing co-operation.

Similarly, differences in the organisation of ownership and regulatory structures have had an impact on EU co-operation on energy regulation (see case study on EU energy regulation). In particular, in the past, the lack of an independent regulator in Germany effectively meant that regulatory co-operation had to proceed in its absence. Furthermore, the scope of authority and the instruments available to each regulator varied from country to country, which led to different perceptions as to what competences could and should be shared, what initiatives should be carried out at supra-national level, which degree of harmonisation may be needed and how regulatory diversity should be accommodated. In this specific example, the divergences in regulatory organisation was addressed through successive EU Directives, that have aimed to provide a minimum level of harmonisation for national regulatory structures, although some differences in powers can still impede some areas of co-ordination.

The case study on transboundary water management illustrates the complexity of IRC in a multi-level governance context. Given the number of responsible authorities across all levels of government involved, water governance is already a complex and challenging undertaking at domestic level. Those complexities and challenges multiply and intensify when attempted on a cross-border basis. Co-operation will be hampered by a mismatch of governance responsibilities and capacity between riparian states. In countries where internal co-ordination mechanisms between parts of the national government with responsibilities related to water are weak or unclear (e.g., authorities responsible for agriculture, environment, trade, health and sanitation, energy, regional or sectoral development, and planning), adding a further layer of co-ordination at supra-national level may be challenging.

Legal obstacles to information sharing are presented as recurrent obstacles to co-operation across all IRC case studies. Closely related, the confidentiality of business information remains an important bottleneck, with firms often reluctant to see their product information shared between governments at the pre-market review stage. It is a crucial point in the case of consumer product safety, where although legal constraints have recently been relaxed in some jurisdictions, they still do not allow for full information sharing on consumer product safety issues. In the case of competition enforcement, most national laws do not permit the sharing of confidential information from a competition authority's investigation file. With very few exceptions, the majority of co-operation instruments and agreements in the antitrust field do not permit the exchange of confidential information. Similarly, significant issues arise in the area of banking regulation with respect to legal limitations on information sharing within national jurisdictions, in particular because much of the relevant information will relate to banks' proprietary models for measuring risk or to confidential information relating to clients.

Difficult political economy of regulatory co-operation

The political economy of regulatory co-operation like any co-operation agreement across states and other stakeholders is complex. A number of factors combine. According to Lazer (2001), States may not harmonise because *1)* they are battling over the gains of harmonisation; *ii)* the actual transaction of reaching a compromise is complex, or *iii)* political elites gain political rents from non-harmonisation. In some cases, the co-operation may collapse because it is deemed captured by specific interest and it loses its credibility.

Co-operation will not be sustainable if it is not perceived as mutually beneficial to all participating countries. However, the costs and benefits of IRC may not be spread equally across countries, giving different incentives to partners to co-operate. Some of the benefits may also not be easily appropriable by countries and while IRC may be beneficial overall, countries may not factor in the global good. In addition, when countries work together, there is always the possibility of "free-riding", i.e. that some countries derive the benefits without incurring the cost of co-operating. This may typically happen in a number of environmental issues, including climate change for which the temptation of free-riding is significant and the burden of action does not fall equally on all, prompting discussions of compensation mechanisms. In this context, the Montreal Protocol on substances that deplete the ozone layer is hailed as an example of a successful co-operation that has managed to come up with an effective compensation mechanism for developing countries (OECD, 1994; Levy, 2011).

While countries may choose to co-operate to avoid a "race to the bottom" whereby countries continuously lower their regulatory standards to acquire a competitive edge (Radaelli, 2004), some remain concerned that the process of finding a consensus may lead to settling for the lowest common denominator and generate sub-optimal regulation. The Policy Research Initiative (2004) defines this second "race to the bottom" effect as the erosion of regulatory standards following "economic integration [that] leads governments to reduce the stringency of their regulation until the lowest common denominator prevails, or they pass regulation they have no intention of enforcing". However, the Policy Research Initiative (2004) mentions a number of empirical studies (Harris, 2003; Industry Canada, 2002; Copeland and Taylor, 2004) that find little evidence in support of the race to the bottom hypothesis.

Implementation challenges

Beyond the signing of agreements and the high level commitment to regulatory co-operation, concretely implementing IRC may be strewn with obstacles. This is an area where case studies are helpful to identify the concrete challenges that implementing IRC may generate. Challenges may be related to a difficult enforcement of the IRC agreement or to a lack of effectiveness of the agreement to achieve its objectives. According to Levy (2011), the effectiveness of co-operative arrangements is in turn affected by two factors: on the one hand the comprehensiveness of coverage and, on the other hand, rule credibility. Rule credibility can be further broken down into: *i)* rule process legitimacy; *ii)* monitoring quality; *iii)* enforcement quality; and *iv)* monitoring and enforcement legitimacy.

The water sector provides an illustration of a variety of legally binding agreements that are not enforced in practice for various reasons. Even in the case of MRAs, several authors (for example Verdier, 2011 and Schmidt, 2012) show that despite the official signature, these legally binding agreements may not become operational. The case study on the prudential regulation of banks provides an important example of inadequate enforcement of mutually agreed prudential standards. The difficulties faced by the BCBS in ensuring consistent implementation of standards lie in part in the opacity of banks' practices and partly in the standards themselves: in allowing calculations of risk exposure based on banks' own internal models, it is difficult for observers to assess whether the standards are being applied consistently. In addition, standards are not legally binding and, until the crisis, the BCBS had no formal sanction mechanisms to ensure implementation. Similarly, the case study on the Model Tax Convention highlights the voluntary dimension of the OECD standards as a reason for which the co-operation is not comprehensive in terms of areas covered and country participation – countries are free to adopt parts of the standards and ignore others.

Fragmentation of IRC mechanisms and actors has been highlighted as a major impediment to the effectiveness of co-operation in several case studies, in particular in the transnational private regulation case. In the case of the prudential regulation of banks, the crisis has prompted a recognition of the need to ensure greater co-ordination in financial regulation, but there are relatively low levels of co-ordination between the different committees established in that perspective. In effect, BCBS, IOSCO and IAIS each have a different membership, and each area (securities, banking and insurance) still has its own focus, mandate, and supervisory traditions. Recognition of foreign qualifications provides another example where a multitude of actors are involved already at the national level. In Austria, for example, four different Ministries are in charge. In addition, in many countries, universities are in charge of the recognition of academic degrees. This complexity of the institutional framework may make the co-operation a difficult endeavour: the different actors may have limited incentives to participate in a process of co-operation that limits their negotiation power; they may also perceive the co-operation as threatening the standards that they have set for themselves (OECD, 2012b).

Achieving comprehensiveness in coverage is an important challenge of IRC, and one that is highlighted in several of the IRC case studies. In prudential regulation, one of the main challenges to co-ordination has been to move beyond co-ordination on standard setting and general information sharing between a relatively small group of countries to extend co-ordination to include more countries. The expansion in the wake of the credit crisis to include the G20 countries has brought all the major economies into the decision making, but its membership is still considerably narrower than that of IOSCO and IAIS. The mismatch between this narrow membership and the fact that prudential standards are adopted globally has led to a number of issues and strong criticisms from developing countries on the applicability of standards to them and the consultation process. The case study on chemical safety highlights the shift in chemical production from OECD countries to non-members as a trend that can potentially threaten the comprehensiveness of the co-operation and makes the OECD less representative and less influential.

Mapping the benefits and challenges with various IRC forms

Beyond the generic benefits and challenges of IRC highlighted in the literature and identified above, there is a need to map the strong points and weaknesses of each specific approach to IRC. Table 2.2 initiates the work by providing a summary of lessons learnt building on the literature and the IRC case studies. More work is needed to develop a truly operational toolkit that would provide guidance on which IRC form may be the most relevant for each situation.

Table 2.2. Advantages and disadvantages of various IRC forms

Type of mechanism	Advantages	Disadvantages
Integration / harmonisation	The rules are the same for all. Compliance is the greatest. Supranational modes of governance are less likely to regulatory capture than networked forms (Kahler and Lake, 2011).	Long process. Costs of the structure and of enforcement. Extensive delegation may be perceived as threatening the popular legitimacy of the mechanism.
Regulatory partnerships between countries	High-level engagement provides a strong signal that supports greater co-operation at lower levels (between regulators). Evidence that such partnerships avoid race to the bottom type of effects. Co-operative agreement that provides a flexible mechanism to address necessary evolution in the partnership.	The federal-only nature of the regulatory initiatives may generate difficulty to address regulations at different levels of jurisdiction.

Table 2.2. **Advantages and disadvantages of various IRC forms** (*cont.*)

Type of mechanism	Advantages	Disadvantages
Intergovernmental organisations	Provide platforms to promote continuous dialogue and anticipate emerging issues. Laboratory of co-operation experiments, laying the groundwork for broader and legally binding international agreements.	May be perceived as talk shops where progress is slow to materialise (Braithwaite and Drahos, 2000). Weaknesses in enforcement and compliance.
Regional agreements with regulatory provisions	Legal force and direct connection to trade and economic integration. Regional agreements offer deeper levels of integration and a higher degree of co-operation than bilateral agreements. They offer economies of scale in enforcement.	May lead to a proliferation of provisions with limited consistency.
Area-specific legally binding agreements	Legal force	Lack of enforcement in some cases. Bilateral agreements may not be sufficient to ensure proper co-operation where multilateral co-ordination is needed (tax matters).
MRA (mutual recognition agreements)	Preserve State sovereignty in rule making and induces minimal adjustment costs. Reduce duplication efforts. May constitute a useful precursor to harmonisation.	The time and cost required to negotiate MR agreements can be high. MRAs require broadly similar regimes and extensive trust between parties and discussions every time changes occur in regulations in one of the co-operating party. Lack of enforcement (some MRAs between the EU and the United States are not enforced). Robust mechanisms need to be established and maintained to deal with disputes.

Table 2.2. Advantages and disadvantages of various IRC forms (*cont.*)

Type of mecanism	Advantages	Disadvantages
Transgovernmental networks	Low-cost, flexible and adaptable / scalable structures, which foster experimentation and innovation (Raustalia, 2002; Levy, 2011) Network regulation supports trust building, technical approaches and may help avoid race to the bottom issues (Esty and Geradin, 2001)	Enforcement and monitoring may be limited owing to a lack of legal basis – mainly based on reputational aspects. The informal nature of regulatory networks is likely to mask unequal power relationships and may strengthen the already powerful regulatory powers. May facilitate exclusion and make monitoring and participation by other officials and non-state actors difficult. Technocratic governance risks supporting the development of a regime with little or no public check on administrative action.
Transnational private regulation	International standardisation can lead to standards and references that are globally accepted by all stakeholders. Enforcement based on contracts and market/reputation pressure is effective in global value chains that extend to countries in which the rule of law is not entirely complied with. Allow heavy reliance on private expertise, which is relevant in markets where the pace of technological change is fast and highly technical information is needed for the definition of implementing measures and technical specifications; and private actors are the most informed parties or the best positioned players to solve a given failure.	Proliferation and fragmentation of private schemes (despite the consolidation under way). The standardisation process tends to be slow and to enshrine existing technical practice. Uncertainty on the performance of TPR and on the conditions under which private schemes can constitute a suitable solution to achieve public goals. Lack of accountability mechanisms and under use by TPR of better regulation instruments (Cafaggi, 2012). In some instances, TPR schemes may fail to achieve comprehensiveness and become clubs of specific interest (Levy, 2011).

Table 2.2. Advantages and disadvantages of various IRC forms (*cont.*)

Type of mecanism	Advantages	Disadvantages
Soft law: guidelines, peer review mechanisms	Flexible tools that can be adapted easily to new and emerging areas / issues.	Compliance and enforcement may be difficult. Countries may feel free to adopt parts of the internationally-agreed standards and ignore others.
Informal exchange of information	Low-cost mode of IRC, allowing the sharing of practices and establishing a common understanding and language on issues. It can help build trust among regulators and provides early warning systems. It fosters regulatory transparency and may help reduce compliance and administrative costs. It is especially effective at bringing regulators together in new fields of regulation where common terminology and approaches need building from the onset.	There is a risk that the co-operation never becomes operational and remains a high-level discussion. The lack of implementation and compliance mechanisms may make this co-operation slow moving and frustrated parties may drop off.

Source: OECD elaboration based on the literature survey and the IRC case studies.

In the case of the most comprehensive IRC mechanism, the full integration through supra national institutions, Zuern and Neyer (2005)[3] conclude that "where the functioning and sanctioning are assumed by centralised institutions that make full use of transnational non-governmental actors, as in the case of the EU, compliance is the greatest." However, Kahler and Lake (2011) notes that despite the rapid increase in global economic integration, there is surprisingly little supra-nationalism. Other forms of international governance, such as governmental networks may be preferred to supra-nationalism in light of distributional and institutional conflict that may arise from regulatory co-operation. Kahler and Lake suggest a number of hypotheses to justify why the supranational option may be chosen over other options (see Box 2.2). Generally, the experience of the EU has shown that full harmonisation may in some cases lead to a number of political deadlocks and be too costly in terms of time and quality of policy action, owing to a disproportionate approach compared to the market failure it aims to solve.

Box 2.2. Supra-nationalism *vs.* horizontal IRC, some hypotheses

- The greater the distributional consequences within or between countries, the more likely states are to favour supranational or hierarchical over network forms of governance.

- The greater the authority of the dominant state or the greater the legitimacy attached to its leadership in a particular issue-area, the more likely a hierarchic governance structure will emerge.

- The greater the number of those disadvantaged by a policy relative to those that benefit from the policy, or the more diffuse the costs relative to the gains, the more states will favour network forms of governance composed only of winners.

- The greater the policy bias of a national institution, the more biased will be any new form of global governance created by that institution.

- The more veto players there are, the more likely national governance and ad hoc co-operation remain as the prevailing modes of governance.

- The greater the agenda-setting power of any actor, the more likely we are to observe a shift away from national governance.

- Countries that lack domestic institutions to make commitments credible will borrow credibility by transferring authority to another state or to a supranational institution.

- Dominant states that lack domestic institutions to make credible commitments or those that have a greater need to establish credibility will favour supranational over hierarchical governance structures.

Source: Based on Kahler and Lake (2011), "Economic Integration and Global Governance: Why So Little Supranationalism?", in W. Mattli and N. Woods (eds.), *The Politics of Global Regulation*, Princeton University Press.

In the case of regulatory partnerships between countries, such as presented in the Regulatory Cooperation Council case study, significant senior-level engagement – by both the Canadian Prime Minister and US President in the case of the Canada-U.S. RCC – proves very effective at increasing the pace and scope of regulatory co-operation between both countries. On the other hand, the federal-only nature of the regulatory partnerships is by itself a challenge. It proves difficult to address regulations at two different levels of jurisdiction given the range of actors that need to be involved (provincial/territorial and state levels). Consequently, as an initial step, the RCC is focusing on regulatory issues under exclusive federal jurisdiction.

MRAs, according to Ziegler (2009), help preserve regulatory diversity, an aspect of great concern to many domestic interest groups. MRAs also do not require a full and costly alteration of the entire regulatory system. However, MRAs presuppose a close degree of equivalence and reciprocal confidence in the responsible institutions of the respective countries involved. MRAs may also encounter some issues of enforcement when not embedded in a hierarchical structure (Schmidt, 2012) – for that matter, MRAs in the context of the EU have special features as they are part of a broader vertical governance system that provides a legally binding framework for co-operation amongst member countries. In addition, MRAs are not necessarily a low cost option. They involve substantial time and resources for their negotiations, and to educate the regulators to use them. The Trans-Tasman Mutual Recognition Arrangement scheme provides a good illustration of the achievements and challenges of MRAs applied broadly to different sectors. According to the Review of Mutual Recognition Schemes of the Australia Productivity Commission,[4] MRAs have been effective in increasing the mobility of goods and labour. However, MRAs have proved to operate much less effectively for occupational activities to the extent that differences in occupational standards between jurisdictions still persist.

Transgovernmental networks have emerged as a decentralised solution to the failures of some of the traditional centre of government based approaches and in response to the rapid development of new information technologies. For Slaughter (2000), transgovernmental networks are "the optimal form of organisation for the information Age". For Raustiala (2002), transgovernmental networks of regulators perform a gap filling role where treaties cannot be developed. They are also likely to complement traditional treaty co-operation, by smoothing the negotiation of treaties and making them work better. In effect, transgovernmental networks are low-cost, flexible and adaptable, scalable structures, which foster experimentation and innovation (Raustalia, 2002; Levy, 2011). They are likely to support trust building among regulators based on technical approaches, which may help avoid race to the bottom concerns (Esty and Geradin, 2001). Some authors, however, point to a number of potential shortcomings, including the fact that networks arise in areas of low politics, where international ramifications remain weak. They may reduce transparency, impede political accountability and reinforce the dominance of major economic powers.

Levy (2011) suggests that private collaborative approaches can be highly credible and effective in their enforcement. Enforcement is mainly sought through market signals – including the reputational risk of non-compliance – which may be an extremely effective way to incentivise compliance of participants. It is not always the case, however, as sometimes market signals may not be sufficient to tilt the incentives of participants towards compliance. As a clear downside, Levy (2011) shows that private schemes prove less effective at achieving comprehensiveness of coverage owing to their voluntary, bottom up character. The case study on TPR also makes a strong case for the need for an evaluation of TPR schemes by third parties, and most notably by public policymakers. Potential misalignment between private benefits and social welfare may arise for different reasons. Among others, collective action in private regulatory bodies can aim at socially sub-optimal outcomes; the TPR scheme might generate negative externalities; the scope of the private regulatory scheme might be narrower than the impacts generated by the activity of its participants; or there might be selection problems or lack of monitoring and compliance that lead to the emergence of socially undesirable outcomes.

Factors of success

The success of IRC is a combination of several elements. Some areas lend themselves more easily to co-operation than others and present important IRC opportunities. The proximity of regulatory set up, issues, objectives and preferences between countries is a key determinant of success. Beyond these relatively "exogenous" factors (e.g. the more or less co-operation friendliness of a sector or of a regulatory area and the "initial" regulatory conditions within different countries are a given at one point in time), the design of the co-operation itself and the process through which it is developed will have an important role in determining the success of a co-operation.

There is a vast literature, in the area of political sciences in particular, which investigates the incentives for co-operating and for diverting from co-operation (see Box 2.3 for a sample of the literature on the topic). Together with the empirical evidence on the factors of success drawn from specific co-operation experiences, these approaches can support a greater understanding of how countries can maximise the benefits of regulatory co-operation, avoid or minimise its pitfalls, to make it overall a success. This Section builds on the available evidence to highlight: *i)* the opportunities for IRC; *ii)* the factors of success; and *iii)* some early conclusions in terms of the critical elements of building IRC.

Box 2.3. **Engaging in co-operation: a perspective from the game theory literature**

The last decades have shown that states have responded to the increased economic pressures "through changes in domestic standards and ambitious regulatory cooperation" (Urpelainen, 2009). This trend is accompanied by a high degree of scholarly attention regarding the "why", "how" and "under what circumstances" states and private actors co-operate on economic policy. The literature in this area benefits from highly interdisciplinary contributions from International law, Political economy, International Relations theory, and Regional Integration theory. Regardless of the angle, however, recent research generally points to the intensely political nature of international co-operation (Urpelainen, 2009; Abbott and Snidal, 2000; Mattli and Buthe, 2009; Vogel, 1995). In international co-operation, states are faced with a range of co-ordination problems, largely stemming from the distributive consequences of their co-operation efforts and challenges pertaining to compliance and enforcement. A prominent approach to the incentives and bargaining of states in co-operating (or refusing to co-operate) stems from rationalist institutional theory. Based on the assumption that states impose significant costs and benefits (policy externalities) on each other when realising their preferences, Rationalists use game theory to analyse the strategic interdependence between states. Verdier (2009) offers a compelling illustration of such an approach applied to IRC and describes three distinct scenarios:

In the scenario of **pure co-ordination games**, states share a common interest in co-ordinating their regulatory actions and similar preferences on the way to achieve this co-operation. Assuming that no state has made pre-existing investments into a particular regulatory standard, each state is indifferent between two assumed regulatory rules. All states, however, share an interest in agreeing on a common regulatory standard because it increases joint welfare. One important feature of pure co-ordination games is that the optimal outcome is self-sustaining – that is, once co-ordination is achieved, states lack incentives to deviate from the rule. As a result, co-ordination does not generally require extensive monitoring and enforcement mechanisms but can be achieved through simple agreement. The agreement does not need to be binding in international law, as long as it provides a "focal point" for states to anticipate each other's actions. Thus pure co-ordination games seem particularly amenable to resolution through informal, nonbinding mechanisms such as regulatory networks.

In a **"Battle of the Sexes"** situation, distributive problems arise because "there are multiple self-enforcing agreements or outcomes that two or more parties would all prefer to no agreement, but the parties disagree in their ranking of the mutually preferable agreements" (Fearon, 1998). In a regulatory context, distributive problems frequently arise when states attempt to harmonise their domestic rules to a global standard, because states often have divergent preferences regarding what the global standard should be. These distributive implications make co-operation harder to attain, because each state may attempt to "hold out" at the negotiation stage in the hope that the other will settle for its preferred outcome. Distributive obstacles to international co-operation are often solved through side payments; that is, if the costs and benefits of each alternative rule can reliably be estimated, the "winner" states may agree *ex ante* to compensate the "loser" states to induce them to adopt their preferred solution. These side payments may take a variety of forms, from cash payments to an agreement to follow the other state's preferred rule in a different area of international co-operation. Alternatively, if states lack sufficient information to estimate the relative costs

Box 2.3. **Engaging in co-operation: a perspective from the game theory literature** (*cont.*)

and benefits of each rule, they may build flexibility provisions that allow the agreement to be renegotiated after some time has elapsed and the distributive consequences are revealed. Powerful states may simply use their clout to steer other toward their preferred outcome by threatening unilateral action. Once attained, co-operation may be self-sustaining without the need for elaborate institutional monitoring, dispute-resolution, or enforcement mechanisms.

In a **Prisoner's dilemma** situation, individual states face incentives to renege on the agreed rules and pursue short-term benefits after the co-operative agreement has been reached. This situation may lead to a situation of a "race to the bottom" where states undercut each other's regulations (Lazer, 2001). The answer to this risk of opportunistic defection lies in the dynamics created by repeated iterations of the game. If both states know that the situation will be repeated indefinitely and care enough about future gains, they may develop retaliation strategies that will provide mutual incentives to co-operate and attain the optimal outcome. The success of these strategies depends on several conditions, including the availability of reliable information to participants regarding defections by others, participants' capacity to threaten retaliation credibly, and self-restraint. In such cases, institutional mechanisms can play a central role in facilitating co-operation. An often-cited example is the international trade regime, in which each state benefits from the co-operative outcome in which all states open their markets, but each state would prefer to defect by erecting barriers to trade while others liberalise. Enforcement comes in the form of countermeasures by individual states. The WTO plays a central role in facilitating and maintaining the co-operative outcome, as it mediates the negotiation of clear rules identifying the expected co-operative behaviour, periodically reviews its members' trade policies for possible violations of global rules, provides an impartial dispute-resolution mechanism to authoritatively identify defections, and provides a legal regime governing countermeasures that limits responses by aggrieved states to what is necessary and proportionate.

Game theory approaches have in common that institutions (such as International Organisations, Transnational Regulatory Networks, supranational regimes, etc.) can provide a way to solve or at least mitigate co-ordination problems by providing a favourable context for bargaining, exchanging information, and establishing enforcement and monitoring mechanisms.

Source: OECD elaboration based on a survey of the literature, 2012.

The opportunities for IRC

OECD (1994) suggests that successes of IRC may be associated particularly with the following areas:

- Programmes which are essentially science driven and based on irrefutable facts (e.g. chemical testing); more generally, areas involving technical assessment or measurement and which benefit from shared methodologies;

- Areas which involve global "goods" or "bads", i.e. where problems are transborder in nature (global warming, ozone depletion, banking, etc.) and cannot be solved by individual governments;

- Issues for which there is a strong incentive for co-operation, e.g. an unambiguous commercial or economic motivation – typically trade and international investment –; or where governments can benefit from sharing information, e.g. health and safety areas.

Box 2.4. Considerations for government in identifying the opportunities for IRC

- The extent to which the regulatory problems with which the regulatory organisation deals are similar to those that counterpart regulators in other governments face;

- The extent to which other governments share the same regulatory objectives in a given field and have similar standards for determining whether those objectives have been met;

- The extent to which the problems and probable solutions depend on social, economic and political – as well as technological – conditions that are similar in other countries or regions;

- The extent to which the identification of solutions entails fast-changing technology or fast-changing standards, and thus entails research and development costs that may advantageously be shared;

- The extent to which regulatory rapprochement in the field is desirable in view of the nature and scope of the activities regulated and the kinds of private interests affected;

- The extent to which regulatory rapprochement in the field would permit the useful sharing of technical services – inspection, testing, certification – among national and subnational administrations;

- The extent to which regulatory organisations have confidence in the technical and regulatory skills of counterpart organisations in other governments;

- The pre-existence of bilateral or multilateral intergovernmental frameworks on the regulatory subject in question.

Source: OECD (1994), *Regulatory Co-operation for an Interdependent World*, Chapter 3, OECD Publishing, Paris.

Table 2.3. Successful and challenging IRC, the perception of countries

In which sector(s) or policy area(s) has IRC been most successful?	In what sector(s) or policy areas has IRC been most problematic?
The implementation of harmonised EU aquis (horizontal/sector specific).	In non-harmonised product sectors (such as e.g. foodstuff and the construction area in the EU), where regulatory infrastructures (authorities) vary and systems for conformity assessment are different.
Environment and green growth	In sectors such as agricultural and fishing industry, security, which relate strongly to the historical and cultural backgrounds of each country.
In areas where there is high trade and/or capital flows	Where there are unique local conditions or difficult regulatory problems to solve.
In areas where there is international convergence around generally accepted standards (electrical safety or electro-magnetic compatibility).	For pharmaceutical products because it is a complex and sensitive area, where the risks and consequences of taking wrong decisions are important.
Sectors with greatest IRC potential are those related to telecommunications, environment, international trade and civil law.	For construction goods (where specific local conditions – such as seismic risk – justify that regulations deviate from the international standards).
In "New" sectors where a significant body of regulation does not yet exist.	In "Old" sectors, where regulatory paths are entrenched.
Goods	Services
Human rights	Intellectual property rights is a difficult sector to co-ordinate because of the pace of technological innovation.

Source: Based on answers to the OECD IRC Survey, 2012.

Bermann further notes in Chapter 3 of OECD (1994) that "regulatory consensus is easier to achieve if it is sought earlier rather than later in the process by which regulations are developed. Agreement is more difficult to reach after national regulatory positions have hardened. Moreover, success is more likely with regulatory proposals that are well-focused, concrete and narrowly defined, rather than broad and overly ambitious". Bermann highlights a number of further considerations that can help policy makers identify the opportunities for IRC (see Box 2.4). They have to do with the proximity of context, of regulatory issues and objectives, the intrinsic technical characteristics of the sector or area where the co-operation would take place and the trust that regulators have in each other. Some of these considerations support the assumptions made in the literature based on game theory that "preferences" of states are instrumental in explaining the likelihood of success of their co-operation.

The findings of OECD (1994), both in terms of the sectors that are most amenable to IRC and the considerations in terms of proximity of problems, objectives and vision, are echoed by the answers to the OECD IRC survey (and summarised in Table 2.3). To the question "In which sector(s) or policy area(s) has IRC been most successful?" countries have generally mentioned areas where technical standards exist – which would fit under Category 1 of the classification above –; areas such as environment and green growth (typical of Category 2 above); and trade in goods (Category 3). By contrast, sectors or areas where there are unique local conditions, difficult regulatory problems to solve and important intangible benefits – typically agriculture, food, service, or intellectual property rights are proving a difficult context for IRC. Similar to the argument already pointed out in OECD (1994), countries find that co-operation is easier in relatively new fields of regulation because a joint understanding of what and how to regulate can develop in the various jurisdictions that co-operate through dialogue. Conversely, in sectors or areas where regulatory paths are already entrenched, it may already be difficult to reconcile positions.

Towards a checklist of critical considerations for successful co-operation

OECD (1994) and others have identified a number of successful and less successful experiences of IRC. Among the failures, the International Convention for the Regulation of Whaling supported by the International Whaling Commission is often flagged as an example of regulatory capture by the industry. By contrast, the Montreal Protocol on substances that deplete the ozone layer is regarded as a successful case of environmental agreement. Levy (2011) confirms this finding and defines the Montreal Protocol as "illustrating powerfully the institutional arrangements that underpin an effective global treaty". A variety of features of the treaty explains its success at achieving comprehensiveness of coverage and rule credibility:

- Enforcement was directly tied to a trade ban.

- The treaty came into effect only after it had been signed by countries representing two thirds of global consumption.

- There was certainty of the scientific fact and the possibility of monitoring of the banned substance.

- Financial support helped developing countries make the transition to CFC alternatives (developed countries committed USD 3 billion to cover the implementation of the Protocol by developing countries).

Box 2.5. **Lessons learnt on the conditions of success in the area of chemical safety**

Several factors combine to explain the success of regulatory co-operation in the chemical safety area. The case study highlights three in particular:

The building of trust among regulators. This took three dimensions: the development of common language/formats, the alignment of testing methods and laboratory practices (through the development of the OECD Guidelines for the Testing of Chemicals and the OECD Principles of Good Laboratory Practice) and the establishment of "binding" Council Acts on Mutual Acceptance of Data.

The progressive growth of a focused initiative. OECD's work began in 1971 with a focus on specific industrial chemicals known to pose health or environmental problems, such as mercury and CFCs. Then, from mid-1970s, the OECD began developing harmonised tools that countries could use to test and assess the risks of (all) new chemicals before they were manufactured and marketed. Once member countries had established workable systems for managing the safety of new chemicals, their attention turned to already existing chemicals. To further facilitate work sharing, OECD then turned to harmonising industry dossiers for the registration of new pesticides, or re-registration of existing pesticides.

Strong industry buy-in and support. The chemicals industry – which includes industrial chemicals, pharmaceuticals, pesticides, biocides, food and feed additives and cosmetics – is one of the world's largest industrial sectors and many chemicals are produced and traded internationally. In 2009, global sales amounted to USD 3.5 trillion and exports to USD 1.5 trillion. Harmonisation of regulations and practices was clearly seen as a way to minimise the variety of regulatory requirements weighting on business and therefore strongly pushed by the industry.

Source: OECD Case study on chemical safety, 2012.

The OECD IRC case studies also provide important insights on the conditions of success of IRC in specific areas of co-operation that are reflected in Boxes 2.5 and 2.6. Box 2.7 explains how the High-level Regulatory Council between Mexico and the United States has followed good regulatory policy principles in the development of the co-operative agreement itself. Based on these results and a number of guidance documenting the steps and ways of strengthening IRC,[5] this report then highlights a number of critical elements or considerations for government to ensure the success of IRC. Further work is needed to refine and complete this preliminary checklist so that it could become an operational tool in support of governments' efforts to develop and strengthen IRC.

Box 2.6. **Lessons learnt on the conditions of success in the area of transboundary water management**

Water provides an interesting case of a sector that has seen both a number of failures and successes in co-operation. Various studies have dealt with the conditions of successful co-operation in the water sector. These conditions, detailed in the case study on transboundary water management, include:

- Political stability and commitment.

- Water governance capacity at national level.

- Strong institutional structure at the transboundary and regional level including common system of data collection and measurement; common terminology; legal framework for agreements between riparian states; and the creation of a multi-member river-basin institution involving all riparian states to implement the agreement with a clear mandate, adequate funding, strong powers for joint monitoring and dispute resolution mechanisms.

- Appropriate human capacity, notably multidisciplinary teams to raise understanding of the complexities of managing shared water resources.

- Creation of a system for sharing costs and benefits, including payments where necessary.

- Adequate financing, both to cover the operating costs of the institutional structure but more substantially to finance the measures which need to be taken.

- Third party facilitation and support, particularly where there is tension over the use of shared water resources.

- Public participation and co-operative working with other bodies at the governmental and non-governmental level and major stakeholders including funding bodies, research organisations, NGOs, local communities and civil society groups, and individual water users and/or influential individuals at the local level.

Source: OECD case study on transboundary water management, 2012.

Box 2.7. **The United States-Mexico High-Level Regulatory Cooperation Council (HLRCC)**

The implementation of the HLRCC is an example of the regulatory governance cycle recommended by the OECD, which considers the following stages for a regulatory process: Planning, Public Consultation, Design, Implementation, Monitoring and Evaluation. The regulatory governance cycle has been a central piece in structuring the Council's work and pushing its agenda forward. In particular, the chronology of the development of the HLRC followed closely the different phases of the governance cycle:

Box 2.7. The United States-Mexico High-Level Regulatory Cooperation Council (HLRCC) (*cont.*)

Initial Presidential Declaration: On May 19th 2012, Presidents Felipe Calderón of México and Barack Obama of the U.S. directed the creation of the "United States – Mexico High Level Cooperation Council", with the purpose of establishing a regulatory co-operation mechanism that would facilitate the development of more efficient regulation, reduce unnecessary transaction costs for commerce, and foster investment between both countries.

Terms of Reference (Planning): Following the creation of the Council, representatives from both countries developed the HLRCC's guiding document, the Terms of Reference (ToR), which were finished on 3 March 2011. The ToR call for an annual work plan addressing regulatory co-operation activities that share two characteristics: high economic impact and political feasibility. The identification of activities was to be based on inputs obtained from the proposals received through a public consultation process in both countries.

Public Consultation: The public consultation process took place in the U.S. from 3 March to 18 April 2011 and led to the submission of 48 proposals for regulatory co-operation. In Mexico it took place from 14 April to 16 May 2011, and led to 252 proposals.

Analysis of Regulatory Cooperation Proposals (Design): Based on the criteria established by the ToR, officials from the Council's co-ordinating offices from each country worked co-operatively to analyse and select regulatory co-operation proposals. This collaboration included the participation of the relevant regulatory agencies for each proposal.

Work Plan Publication (Implementation): The Council's first annual Work Plan was published on February 28th 20?2. It includes seven regulatory co-operation activities with a series of deliverables to be accomplished during the annual timeframe of the Work Plan. It also establishes working groups co-chaired by the relevant regulatory agencies from each country, which are responsible for accomplishing the deliverables in seven regulatory co-operation activities included in the Work Plan.

Follow up on the activities of the Work Plan (Implementation and Monitoring): After the publication of the Work Plan, the activities of each working group have been monitored by the Council's co-ordinating offices in each country. This has been done by periodically updating a simple report by each working group which includes intermediate actions required to complete the Work Plan deliverables. The Council's co-ordinating offices arranged for conference calls between each working group, to ensure that specific issues are discussed and solutions defined in order to deliver results.

Evaluation of the progress of the Work Plan and the Regulatory Cooperation process (Evaluation): The Council is preparing for an evaluation session involving the participation of High-Level Officials from each country. In this meeting, the progress of each of the working groups will be analysed in order to improve the efficacy of the Council.

Source: Vice-Ministry for Competitiveness and Standardization of Mexico, and the Office of Management and Budget of the United States (2012).

High level political commitment to ensure leadership and oversight

According to the Policy Research Initiative (2004), "Political commitment is necessary to overcome implementation hurdles arising from agreements requiring internal co-operation between two or more organisations, when organisational mandates are incompatible, or when sub-national governments share responsibility for delivering regulatory results. A strong political commitment can also help reconcile potentially conflicting national interests and international opportunities". The case study on the RCC highlights the importance of senior-level engagement on this initiative in increasing the pace and scope of regulatory co-operation between both countries. While regulator-to-regulator contact had always been a hallmark of the Canada-US relationship, a lack of sustained focus at senior levels of both governments had in the past failed to address more systemic barriers to collaboration.

Conversely, one of the key challenges to the development of the Global Risk Assessment Dialogue has been maintaining the momentum in the absence of clear high level political support. The initiative grew from the 'bottom up' – from the interest and commitment of individuals particularly within the EU Commission (DG SANCO), and agencies in the United States and Canada – and has not yet received higher political commitment. It therefore lacks political momentum and organisational infrastructure to ensure that resources are allocated to the project, and that clear timelines and deliverables are set. Similarly, Australia and New Zealand Productivity Commissions (2012) highlights the risk related to the current decentralised model of the Australia/New Zealand Closer Economic Relations governance and in particular the fact that there is no single government body "responsible for setting the overall agenda, overseeing the relationship and monitoring progress and performance". The recommendation is to "create a clearer leadership and oversight role for CER, building on existing governance arrangements and the annual meeting of Prime Ministers".

Embedding IRC in regulatory processes

In line with the 2012 OECD *Recommendation of the Council on Regulatory Policy and Governance*, greater consideration should be given to all relevant international standards and frameworks for co-operation when developing regulatory measures. This would ensure that governments take into account relevant international regulatory environment when formulating regulatory proposals; act in accordance with their international treaty obligations; and avoid the duplication of efforts in regulatory activity in cases where recognition of existing regulations and standards would achieve the same public interest objective at lower costs. Along these lines, the

Australia and New Zealand Productivity Commissions (2012) recommend that "When significant new regulatory proposals or modifications arise at the national level, the responsible government agencies should examine opportunities for trans-Tasman and/or broader collaboration that would lower costs and deliver net benefits".

Reciprocally, the evidence collected for this report points to the fact that IRC mechanisms do not systematically make use of good regulatory policy governance and tools, such as RIAs, *ex post* evaluation or appropriate consultation. In this respect, the EU and New Zealand/Australia co-operation provide references for the use of RIAs in the rule-making process. The Mexico-US HLRCC is also an example of the regulatory governance cycle recommended by the OECD. Based on these examples, more systematic adoption of good regulatory policy principles and tools in the development and management of IRC by countries and by international institutions with regulatory powers (including IGO, international standard-setting bodies and inter-governmental networks) would help increase the accountability of these organisations and improve the quality of their rule making processes. The OECD *Recommendation of the Council on Regulatory Policy and Governance* could provide the guidance of reference for scaling up regulatory policy at cross-jurisdictional level.

Establishing appropriate consultation mechanisms

Public consultation and the involvement from the outset and support of the potentially regulated entities and of a broader range of stakeholders can contribute to focusing action where needed, to forging a consensus that will support implementation and to ensuring accountability of the IRC mechanism. Both the Regulatory Cooperation Council between Canada and the United States and High-level Regulatory Council between Mexico and the US have relied strongly on stakeholder engagement to design the co-operation itself. In the case of the RCC, stakeholder engagement helped to identify elements in the Action Plan and to support the development of detailed Work Plans. In the case of the HLRC (Box 2.7), public consultation has helped to identify 48 proposals for regulatory co-operation in the United States and 252 proposals in Mexico. In the case of the recognition of foreign qualifications, the involvement of all actors that have a stake in the process, including employers, has been flagged as a key factor of success.

Building trust among regulators

Trust is central to building co-operative relationships between regulatory authorities. This is well illustrated in the different IRC case studies. The case study on competition shows that a lack of trust – caused by a weak legal framework in the country seeking co-operation, insufficient transparency of the competition authority's procedures or inadequate safeguards for due process – heightens perceptions that information may be leaked, putting the investigations of foreign authorities at risk and undermining the effectiveness of their cartel enforcement programmes and associated tools. There may be a lack of confidence in the ability of the requested country to provide information of the quality and/or standard necessary for the requesting country to use it in its own investigation. This is a higher risk with newer competition authorities (but this can be applied more generally to regulatory authorities) that have not yet established the necessary safeguards or acquired sufficient experience to handle such requests, which constitutes a real obstacle for co-operation between countries with mature competition authorities and new and less experienced competition regimes.

The case study on chemical safety shows the value of forums, as provided by the OECD to exchange technical and policy information. By discussing their chemical control policies together, countries tend to develop similar policies and regulations and have greater confidence in each other's systems. In the case of chemical safety, this has culminated in the development of Test Guidelines and Principles of Good Laboratory Practice. These tools, developed through consensus in the OECD realm, underpin the Mutual Acceptance of Data (MAD) system – under which chemical safety data developed using OECD Test Guidelines and OECD principles of Good Laboratory Practice in one Member country must be accepted in all member countries. They therefore constitute (with the enforcement mechanisms) the foundations of the system of trust upon which regulatory co-operation is based.

Common language, baseline – through taxonomy, classifications

Common language and definition contribute to trust building and form the foundations of collaborative relations. This is again well documented throughout the case studies. In water, studies have found that the exercise of building common data sets and engaging in joint monitoring improve co-operation for transboundary water management. In the 1992 Helsinki Convention on transboundary water, this has notably taken the form of an emphasis being placed on the development of common systems of data collection, analysis and presentation. In chemical safety, this has taken the form of the development and implementation of the Global System of Harmonisation of Classification and Labelling – a joint effort by OECD, ILO and UNITAR. Similarly, one of the goals pursued by the adoption, in 1963, of the first OECD Model Tax Convention was to achieve a uniform interpretation of the standard provisions included in this model to reduce potential conflicts between tax authorities of different countries concerning the meaning of these provisions. With regards to consumer product safety, the development of a global product taxonomy was seen as essential to support better sharing of information across jurisdictions and tracking of unsafe products across borders.

Overcoming the constraints to and promoting the exchange of information

Sharing information appears as the first and essential step in regulatory co-operation (as well as one of its outcomes). The issues of legal obstacles to information sharing and of confidentiality of business information have been identified in this report and supporting case studies as recurring bottlenecks to IRC. Clearly identifying the constraints to information exchange and establishing platforms and other mechanisms to overcome those constitute critical steps to successful co-operation. It is one of the main objectives and a crucial mandate of regulatory networks. In the case of the recognition of foreign qualifications, for instance, the ENIC-NARIC network was originally established to share information about qualifications. In the area of competition enforcement, cooperation is largely based on tools such as waivers of confidentiality that companies subject to an investigation grant to authorities, allowing them to exchange confidential information on the case.

Going further and providing a "joint" platform – typically through a web interface – may further facilitate the sharing of information of cross-jurisdictional interest. In relation to OECD co-operation on product safety, the focus has been clearly put on supporting the safety of consumer products in global markets through better information exchange within and between economies and through the development of systematic methods for monitoring developments in consumer product safety, notably in policy and enforcement. A 10-point action plan has been developed that prioritises the development of a global portal on product recalls and an inventory of international and national consumer product safety initiatives. The former is aimed at an automatic and timely gathering of information on unsafe products from domestic web sites into a single OECD platform and the latter at provision of a web space for exchange of information on ongoing and upcoming activities in the consumer product safety area. Shortly, work could begin on a longer term project to develop a common framework for injury data collection and dissemination. Currently, there are several jurisdictional or regional based systems that collect injury data on consumer products. There is, however, no single source of this data at a global level.

Ensuring compliance

Putting in place the mechanisms to enforce regulatory co-operation effectively and implement the outcomes of the co-operation has been highlighted throughout the case studies as a critical element of IRC. In the assessment of the mixed results of the co-operation in prudential regulation of banks, shortcomings have been identified in relation to monitoring and implementation. Co-ordination between member countries as to their implementation of BCBS standards in national law and supervisory practice used to be mainly carried out through surveys. Since the crisis, the Basel Committee has also adopted a much firmer stance on implementation of standards in the area of bank supervision. Until the crisis, it aimed at providing a forum for information sharing and co-operation between supervisors, with the view that through such exchanges, consistent practices would develop and be implemented at national level. It relied mainly on national supervisors to implement the standards. Since the crisis, however, mechanisms have been added, such as the provision of standard interpretations of the Basel Accords, and peer reviews overseen by the Standards Implementation Group (a subcommittee of BCBS). There is also a move to monitor implementation by investigating banks directly, rather than addressing their activities at national supervisors.

The EU energy regulatory framework has shown a similar trend towards more stringent enforcement mechanisms. In this specific case, diverging interests and market structures across jurisdictions have made it difficult for member states to act in the interests of the EU region as a whole, when this would not also provide direct benefit to their own country (EU Commission 2011b). Consequently, co-operation on energy regulation within the EU has become increasingly formalised over the last 10-15 years. This gradual process has had three key characteristics: *i)* increased legalisation, *ii)* increased development of formal institutional structures for co-ordination; and *iii)* a shift of power from national to the supranational level.

Sharing costs and benefits

The IRC case studies have shown that market structure and other structural elements were critical for understanding the gains and costs incurred by countries through IRC, their incentives to co-operate and the need for compensation mechanisms. In transboundary water management, for instance, depending on the position of the country in the river basin, incentives to co-operate vary substantially. Based on UN-Water (2008) and Dieperink (2011), the case study suggests ways of overcoming the diverging interests through the development of a consensus over basic entitlements and of a management plan which pays attention to the differential distribution of costs resulting from the use of water resources over the entire river basin and which maximises overall benefits. The case study also mentions possible payments for benefits (or compensation for costs), although as of today a consensual methodology does not exist. It also suggests adopting special approaches with respect to benefits and costs that are not easily quantifiable or commensurable, such as for flood mitigation, regulating run-off and water supply.

Evaluation

Regular reviews of the co-operation are essential to ensure its effectiveness. This has been a major conclusion in the case of the Australia/New Zealand Closer Economic Relations that "The Australian and New Zealand Governments should undertake five-yearly public reviews of CER to take stock of what has been achieved and learnt, and ensure that the agenda remains relevant and forward looking" (Australia and New Zealand Productivity Commissions, 2012). Similarly, in the HLRCC case, the evaluation of the progress of the Work Plan and the Regulatory Co-operation process is flagged as a key pillar (see Box 2.7).

Incorporate flexibility mechanisms to continuously adapt to changing market structure and new issues.

IRC takes time to develop and needs perpetual adjustments. A success may become obsolete if there is no mechanism in place to accommodate emerging issues. The evolution in the focus of the co-operation on tax matters within the OECD is a good illustration of this need for constant adaptation. From the 1920s to the early 1980s, co-ordination efforts were primarily directed at developing the network of bilateral tax treaties through the drafting of standard provisions to help the negotiation and conclusion of bilateral tax treaties. In the early 1980s, the co-ordination efforts of the OECD and its member countries started to focus a lot more on the interpretation and application of existing treaties. The co-ordination efforts have gradually moved from improving market access (through the removal of double taxation) towards conflict avoidance and resolution and facilitating the inter-operability of tax systems. Over the last 10 years, there has been another shift in the main objective of the co-ordination towards improved transparency and exchange of information in tax matters. Similarly, the evolution of the International Commission for the Protection of the Rhine illustrates this need for continual adaptation of the co-ordination mechanism. Effective evolution may be supported by periodic reviews and assessments followed by adaptations and modifications in goals or strategies to meet changing circumstances or opinions (Huisman, de Jong and Wieriks, 2000).

Chemical safety is a domain where IRC is relatively advanced compared to others. Consequently, the challenges faced reflect this level of advancement and, most importantly, shed light on the difficulties that a dynamic co-operation may generate. Because of the shift over the years in chemical production from OECD countries to non-members, the initial forum that was mainly comprised of OECD countries has become less representative and less influential in the global setting over the years. Involving new players has therefore become a critical step to preserve the balance of interests in the co-operation, but may involve important challenges. A second consequence of the maturity of the co-operation for the control of chemicals is that many of the "easy" issues have been dealt with and the technical complexity (including advancements in science) of the remaining tasks increases. With increased complexity of issues and increased number of players involved, the process of obtaining consensus may become slower.

Table 2.4. Benefits from IRC as identified in the IRC case studies

	Chemical safety	Consumer product safety	EU energy regulation	Model Tax Convention	Transboundary water management	Prudential regulation of banks
Economic efficiency	Level the playing field for the industry.		Market competition through liberalisation and the development of an efficient internal market.			Provide minimum standards, regulatory harmonisation to ensure a 'level playing field' for internationally active banks.
Reduced costs on economic activity	Avoid duplication of testing, saving resources for industry and society. Reduction in delays for marketing new products				Increased food and energy production (reduced costs of inputs for business).	
Increased trade and investment flows	Minimise non-tariff barriers to trade, which might be created by differing test methods required among countries	Reduced obstacles on trade in products.		Abolition of double taxation, an important obstacle to cross-border trade and investment		

Table 2.4. Benefits from IRC as identified in the IRC case studies (cont.)

	Chemical safety	Consumer product safety	EU energy regulation	Model Tax Convention	Transboundary water management	Prudential regulation of banks
Progress in managing risks and global goods across borders	Better health and environment protection through greater evaluation of chemicals and action taken	More efficient & effective detection and reaction on consumer product safety issues within & across jurisdictions lead to reduced number of injuries.	Security of supply by facilitating the movement of electricity and gas within the EU and between EU and neighbouring states		Political security and regional integration. Better ecological management and environmental sustainability, through cross-border management of pollution risks. Better management of risks to human health and security (such as loss of life in the event of floods).	Ensure global financial stability and avoid global systemic risks.
Greater transparency	Increased availability of safety data on high production volume chemicals	Greater exchange of information on product safety within and between economies;		Improve transparency and exchange of information in tax matters. This has led to the elimination of bank secrecy as an obstacle to the effective exchange of information upon request.		

Table 2.4. Benefits from IRC as identified in the IRC case studies *(cont.)*

	Chemical safety	Consumer product safety	EU energy regulation	Model Tax Convention	Transboundary water management	Prudential regulation of banks
More efficient administrative relations (e.g. clearer and less contentious)	Exchange of information and practices between countries with different policy experience. Development of common language through harmonised classification and labelling systems for chemical products	Improved quality and effectiveness of regulation through exchange of information, access to good regulatory practices and more co-ordinated action.		Flexible co-ordination which facilitates the relations between tax administrations whilst preserving the tax sovereignty of countries involved.		
Other	Reduce the use and suffering of laboratory animals needed for toxicological tests.	Support research on product safety issues	EU solidarity	Uniform interpretation of tax treaties allows a reduction in conflicts between taxpayers and tax authorities.	Food security and poverty alleviation	

Source: Case studies on chemical safety; consumer product safety; OECD Model Tax Convention; EU energy regulation; prudential regulation of banks; and transboundary water management, 2012.

Table 2.5. Challenges raised by IRC as identified in the case studies

	Chemical safety	Consumer product safety	EU Energy regulation	Competition enforcement	Model Tax Convention	Transboundary water management	Prudential regulation of banks
Lack of regulatory flexibility			Differences in regulatory structures have made IRC difficult. Ex: In the past, lack of a regulator in Germany or variation in scope of authority, competences, instruments available to each regulator.	Differences in how competition authorities or courts define confidential information in cartel cases and whether cartels are criminally prosecuted.		Differences between riparian countries in terms of socio-economic development; governance capacities; technical infrastructure; legal frameworks; political & cultural orientations; data collection, measurement and assessment.	

Table 2.5. Challenges raised by IRC as identified in the case studies (*cont.*)

	Chemical safety	Consumer product safety	EU Energy regulation	Competition enforcement	Model Tax Convention	Transboundary water management	Prudential regulation of banks
Legal obstacles (restrictions on information sharing/ confidentiality rules)		Legal constraints to sharing information		Most national laws do not permit the sharing of confidential information from a competition authority's investigation file, nor do they permit an authority to use its compulsory gathering powers on behalf of a foreign competition authority	The incorporation of tax treaties into domestic law may raise country-specific constitutional & legal issues. The independence of the judicial branch and the fact that judges are not represented in international fora dealing with tax treaties make it difficult to achieve co-ordination in the way domestic courts interpret tax treaties provisions.	Lack of co-ordination between parts of the national government with responsibilities related to water (e.g. between ministries, or public agencies.	Legal limitations on information sharing within national jurisdictions, in particular because much of the relevant information will relate to banks' proprietary models for measuring risk and client confidentiality.

Table 2.5. **Challenges raised by IRC as identified in the case studies** (*cont.*)

	Chemical safety	Consumer product safety	EU Energy regulation	Competition enforcement	Model Tax Convention	Transboundary water management	Prudential regulation of banks
Unequal distribution of costs and benefits within and across countries			Different interests, risks, costs and benefits of member states arising from different ownership structures, industry structures and different positions in the energy supply chain			Competition for a scarce resource; conflicts of interest and priorities; negative externalities of the actions of one riparian country on another, for example construction of dams or hydro-electric power stations, pollution from upstream jurisdiction.	

Table 2.5. Challenges raised by IRC as identified in the case studies (*cont.*)

	Chemical safety	Consumer product safety	EU Energy regulation	Competition enforcement	Model Tax Convention	Transboundary water management	Prudential regulation of banks
Administrative costs of IRC	Budgetary constraints	Sufficient resources will be required to continuously maintain the portal on product recalls and inventory of initiatives.		Co-operation can be resource intensive, distracting scare resource from other enforcement activities.			
Other	Need for continual adjustment in a context where "easy" issues have been dealt with.	Avoiding duplication of work taking place in other global fora			Countries are free to adopt parts of the standards and ignore others IRC is not comprehensive in terms of areas covered & country participation.	Lack of personnel with requisite skills Lack of adequate data collection, monitoring and enforcement systems Lack of adequate financing.	Inclusion of more countries. Implementation of and day to day supervision.

Source: Case studies on chemical safety; consumer product safety; OECD Model Tax Convention; EU energy regulation; prudential regulation of banks; and transboundary water management, 2012.

Notes

1. As with all perception surveys, these survey results have to be considered with caution. They cannot be taken as reflecting a wide consensus within government and are difficult to make a cross-country comparison.

2. In January 2013, for instance, the new president of the Nordic Council claimed that "It's time the north of Europe had a stronger voice in Europe", www.norden.org/en/news-and-events/news/its-time-the-north-of-europe-had-a-stronger-voice-in-europe.

3. The study examines several regulatory arenas (EU; WTO/GATT, national, inter-Laender system in Germany) in three different regulatory fields (subsidy control, trade in foodstuffs, and redistributional mechanisms).

4. www.pc.gov.au/projects/study/mutual-recognition-schemes.

5. They involve: the ACUS Recommendation (from the US Administrative Conference, 2011www.acus.gov/research/the-conference-current-projects/international-regulatory-cooperation); the Guidelines on International Regulatory Obligations and Cooperation (2007) of the Treasury Board of Canada, which interpret the policy requirements in the Cabinet Directive on Streamlining Regulation pertaining to international obligations and international regulatory cooperation (www.tbs-sct.gc.ca/ri-qr/documents/gl-ld/iroc-cori/iroc-cori-eng.pdf); the Guidelines on Regulatory cooperation and Transparency in support of the EU – US regulatory cooperation (http://ec.europa.eu/enterprise/policies/international/files/guidelines3_en.pdf); and OECD (1994), Chapter on "Strategies for expanding regulatory co-operation".

Bibliography

Abbott, K. and D. Snidal (2000), "Hard and Soft Law in International Governance", *International Organization,* Vol. 54, No. 3, pp. 421-456.

Andriamanajara S. *et al.* (2004), "The Effects of Non-Tariff Measures on Prices, Trade and Welfare: CGE Implementation of Policy-Based Price Comparisons", U.S International Trade Commission, *Office of Economics Working Paper* No. 2004-04.A.

Ahearn (2009), *Transatlantic Regulatory Cooperation: Background and Analysis*, CRS Report for the US Congress.

Australia and New Zealand Productivity Commissions (2012), "Strengthening trans-Tasman Economic Relations", Discussion Draft, September.

Braithwaite, J. and P. Drahos (eds.) (2000), *Global Business Regulation*, Cambridge University Press, Cambridge.

Cafaggi F. (2011), "New Foundations of Transnational Private Regulation", *Journal of Law and Society*.

Cafaggi F. (2012), "The Regulatory Function of Transnational Commercial Contracts: New architectures", European University Institute – Department of Law (LAW).

Chen, M.X., T. Otsuki, J.S. Wilson (2006), "Do Standards Matter for Export Success?", *Policy Research Working Papers*, No. 3809, World Bank, Washington, DC.

Copeland, B. and M. Taylor (2004), "Trade, Growth, and the Environment", *Journal of Economic Literature,* Vol. 42, pp. 7-71.

Copenhagen Economics (2009), "Assessment of Barriers to Trade and Investment between the EU and Japan", report prepared for the European Commission, DG Trade, Copenhagen.

Dee, P. et al. (2011), "The Impact of Trade Liberalisation on Jobs and Growth: Technical Note", *OECD Trade Policy Working papers*, No. 107, OECD Publishing, Paris.

Dierx, I. and H. Schmidt (2005), *Competition, Regulatory Cost and Economic Growth*.

Drezner, D. (2007), *All Politics is Global,* Princeton University Press, Princeton.

ECORYS (2009), *Non-Tariff Measures in EU-US Trade and Investment – An Economic Analysis*, Report commissioned by the European Commission.

Esty D.C. and D. Geradin (2000), "Regulatory Co-opetition", *Journal of International Economic Law*, Vol. 3, Issue 2, pp. 235-255, Oxford.

EU (1985), Council Resolution on a new approach to technical harmonisation and standards.

Commission of the European Communities (1985), Completing the Internal Market, White Paper from the Commission to the European Council, (COM(85)310 final).

Fearon, J. (1998), "Bargaining, Enforcement, and International Cooperation", *International Organization*, Vol. 52, Issue 2, pp. 269-305.

Griffith, R., R. Harrison and H. Simpson (2006), *Product Market Reform and Innovation in the EU*, The Institute for Fiscal Studies.

Harris, R. (2003), "North American Linkages: Opportunities and Challenges for Canada", *The Industry Canada Research Series*, Vol. 11. University of Calgary Press, Calgary.

Hood, C. (2002), "The Risk Game and the Blame Game" *Government and Opposition*, Vol. 37, Issue 1, pp. 15-37.

Howse, R. (2004), "Transatlantic Regulatory Co-operation and the Problem of Democracy", in: George A. Bermann et al. (eds.), *Transatlantic Regulatory Co-operation. Legal Problems and Political Prospects*, Oxford University Press, Oxford.

Huisman P., J. de Jong and K. Wieriks (2000) "Transboundary cooperation in shared river basins: experiences from the Rhine, Meuse and North Sea", in *Water Policy 2*, pp. 83-97.

Industry Canada (2002), "International Regulatory Co-operation", quoted in Policy Research Initiative.

Kahler, M. and D. Lake (2011), "Economic Integration and Global Governance: Why So Little Supranationalism?", in W. Mattli and N. Woods (eds.), *The Politics of Global Regulation*, Princeton University Press.

Kawamoto (1997), "Product Standards, Conformity Assessment and Regulatory Reform", in *OECD Report on Regulatory Reform*, Vol. I, OECD Publishing, Paris.

Keohane R. and J. Nye (1974), "Transgovernmental Relations and the International Organisations", *World Politics*, Vol. 26, Issue 1, pp. 39-62.

Koenig-Archibugi, M. (2010), "Global Regulation", in: R. Baldwin et al. (eds.), *The Oxford Handbook of Regulation,* Oxford University Press, Oxford.

Lazer, D. (2001), "Regulatory interdependence and international governance", *Journal of European Public Policy*, Vol. 8, Issue 3, pp. 474-492.

Levy B. (2011), "Innovations in Globalised Regulation", *Policy Research Working Paper*, World Bank.

Licht, A. (1999), "Games Commissions Play: 2x2 Games of International Securities Regulation", *The Yale Journal of International Law*, Vol. 24, pp. 61-125.

Mattli, W. and T. Buthe (2003), "Setting International Standards: Technological Rationality or Primacy of Power?", *World Politics,* 56(1), pp. 1–42.

Mattli, W. and N. Woods (eds.) (2009), *The Politics of Global Regulation*, Princeton University Press.

Meuwese A. (2009), "EU-U.S. Horizontal Regulatory Cooperation", Paper for the California-EU Regulatory Cooperation Project Leuven, Conference Brussels, 10 June.

Mugge, D. (2006), "Private-Public Puzzles: Inter-firm Competition and Transnational Private Regulation", *New Political Economy*, Vol. 11 (2), pp. 177-200.

OECD (2012a), *Recommendation of the Council on Regulatory Policy and Governance*, OECD, Paris.

OECD (2012b), *Jobs for Immigrants (Vol. 3): Labour Market Integration in Austria, Norway and Switzerland*, OECD Publishing. doi: 10.1787/9789264167537-en.

OECD (2011), "The Impact of Trade Liberalisation on Jobs and Growth: Technical Note", *OECD Trade Policy Papers*, No. 107, OECD Publishing. doi: 10.1787/5kgj4jfj1nq2-en.

OECD (2010a), *Transition to a Low-Carbon Economy: Public Goals and Corporate Practices*, OECD Publishing. doi: 10.1787/9789264090231-en.

OECD (2010b), *Cutting Costs in Chemicals Management: How OECD Helps Governments and Industry*, OECD Publishing. doi: 10.1787/9789264085930-en.

OECD (1998), "Regulatory Reform and International Standardisation", Paris.

OECD (1994), *Regulatory Cooperation for an Interdependent World*, OECD Publishing, Paris.

Pettriccione, M. (2000), "Reconciling Transatlantic Regulatory Imperatives with Bilateral Trade", in Bermann et al. (eds.), *Transatlantic Regulatory Co-operation. Legal Problems and Political Prospects*, Oxford University Press, Oxford.

Policy Research Initiative (2004), *Canada-US Regulatory Co-operation: Charting a Path Forward,* Interim report, Canada.

Radaelli C. (2004), *"Markets and Regulatory Competition in Europe"*, *Special issue of Journal of Public Policy*, Vol. 24, Issue 1.

Raustiala, K. (2002), "The Architecture of International Cooperation: Transgovernmental Networks and the Future of International Law", *Virginia Journal of International Law Association*, Vol. 43, Issue 1.

Schmidt, S. (2012), "Transnational governance through mutual recognition", paper prepared for the Conference on the distributional effects of transnational regulation, Rome, May.

Stewart R. (2012), "The enforcement of transnational regulation", in F. Cafaggi (ed.), *The enforcement of transnational regulation*.

The Australia and New Zealand School of Government (n.d.), Arrangements for facilitating trans-Tasman government institutional co-operation, Australia Department of Finance and Administration and New Zealand Ministry of Economic Development.

Urpelainen, J. (2009), "All or Nothing: Avoiding Inefficient Compromise in International Cooperation", Dissertation at the University of Michigan.

Verdier, H. (2009), "Transnational Regulatory Networks and Their Limits", *The Yale Journal of International Law*, Vol. 34, pp. 113-172.

Vogel, D, (1995), *Trading Up: Consumer and Environmental Regulation in a Global Economy,* Harvard University Press, Cambridge.

Wilson J. and C. Mann (2005), "Assessing the Benefits of Trade Facilitation: a Global Perspective", *The World Economy*, Vol. 28, Issue 6, pp 841-871.

World Trade Organisation (2012), *World Trade Report 2012, Trade and Public Policies: A Closer Look at Non-tariff Measures in the 21st Century.*

Ziegler, O. (2009), "EU-US regulatory coordination, A two-level game approach", *Working Papers, des Forums Regensburger Politikwissenschaftler*, FRP Working Paper 04/2009, Regensburg.

Zuern, M. and J. Neyer (2005), "The conditions for compliance", in M. Zuern and C. Joerges (eds.), *Law and Governance in Postnational Europe,* Cambridge University Press, Cambridge.

Conclusion: Areas for further work

As an initial step, this stocktaking report shows the multiplicity of IRC arrangements, the important benefits that can accrue from greater regulatory co-operation, but also the remaining analytical gaps and the complexity of implementing effective IRC. Clearly, more work is needed to guide governments in a number of areas. In that respect, the OECD presents unique advantages to advance the thinking and build a shared understanding on IRC. The OECD can build on its long-standing expertise in promoting regulatory co-operation among its members in various policy areas. It can tap into the experiences of its members in an area where countries and the EU have accumulated substantial experience from which important lessons and good practices can be drawn. The organisation also has the credibility and analytical strength to engage governments in fruitful discussions on a politically sensitive area, by anchoring the debate in evidence-based analysis. It has the convening power to reach out to different communities. Within the OECD, the Regulatory Policy Committee and its *Recommendation on Regulatory Policy and Governance* provide a relevant cross-sectoral framework for anchoring the discussions.

Greater guidance on good IRC practices

Principle 12 of the *OECD Recommendation of the Council on Regulatory Policy and Governance* urges countries to: "In developing regulatory measures, give consideration to all relevant international standards and frameworks for co-operation in the same field and, where appropriate, their likely effects on parties outside the jurisdiction". More guidance is needed to address the challenge that globalisation and the need to regulate across borders are raising for traditional regulatory governance. In this context, the development of a typology of IRC mechanisms would help countries develop a common understanding of the range of IRC options and a common language on IRC in view of facilitating intra-government and transboundary discussions of IRC, as well as providing sound information based on trends in IRC. In the longer run, further work on the benefits, costs and challenges of various IRC options and the development of a checklist of key considerations for developing beneficial co-operation would help to systematise and rationalise decision making on regulatory co-operation. This would also provide governments with evidence-based tools to better understand when and how to seek strengthened international regulatory co-operation.

Good regulatory policy principles for international organisations and transnational regulators

IGOs and other international organisations (public, private and multi-stakeholder) are playing a growing role in supporting regulatory co-operation in multiple areas. They do so through the issuance of more or less binding standards and through various dialogue processes. While these organisations may adopt good regulatory policy principles and practices – such as consultation or regulatory impact assessment – on an ad hoc basis, they do not however systematically refer to regulatory policy tools to support their rule-making processes. Their more systematic adoption could help increase the accountability of these organisations and improve the quality of their rule-making process. Based on its long-standing expertise in the regulatory policy field, the RPC could help by investigating the use of good regulatory policy practices in international organisations and identifying ways at strengthening their uptake.

Towards a framework for the assessment of TPR from the standpoint of public policy

Rare are the sectors or areas where regulatory co-operation is fully public and state-based. In most cases, at least the technical standards used are developed by private standard setters or private organisations. The case study on TPR supports the view that a comprehensive theoretical framework for the assessment of TPR as a possible regulatory alternative from the standpoint of public policy is missing. The conditions under which private schemes could constitute a suitable, reliable way to achieve publicly recognised goals, have not yet been clarified. Focusing more on TPR and national private regulation would bring about three important changes. First, explicit endorsement of existing schemes by national regulators would contribute to their legitimacy and their in-depth scrutiny from the standpoint of public policy. Second, it would force public regulators to develop comparative methodologies to select cases in which private regulation is likely to complement effectively public regulation and at times even to perform better than public regulation, and for which phases of the value chain. Third, it might lead to better guidance to TPR schemes as to what governance arrangements, procedural requirements, regulatory tools and enforcement mechanisms they should adopt in order to meet minimum reliability and legitimacy thresholds from the perspective of society at large.

The role of the OECD in promoting regulatory co-operation through soft law and peer pressure

The OECD has played and continues to play a substantial role in promoting regulatory co-operation in various fields – from environment to product safety and competition issues. However, this role is not necessarily well known (outside of the OECD) and the OECD is sometimes perceived as not being transparent enough on its work and processes. Future work by the RPC could explain the role that a forum like the OECD plays in supporting regulatory co-operation and highlight the processes by which the OECD produces and enforces soft law and complements the efforts of government to promote good regulation.

Annex A

The IRC case studies

A. The choice of case studies

The case studies have been selected to reflect the range of different IRC mechanisms as identified in this report. The table relates the ten case studies to the IRC mechanisms they illustrate.

The Canada-U.S. Regulatory Cooperation Council provides an example of a regulatory partnership between countries. The RCC is an initiative, launched by President Obama and Prime Minister Harper in February 2011, between both federal governments aimed at pursuing greater alignment in regulation, increasing mutual recognition of regulatory practices and establishing smarter, more effective and less burdensome regulations in specific sectors.

The four case studies on chemical safety, consumer product safety, competition law enforcement and co-ordination of bilateral tax treaties provide examples of co-operative agreements developed through the OECD, an intergovernmental organisation promoting regulatory co-operation through soft law. In addition, the case study on chemical safety illustrates the example of a multilateral mutual recognition agreement; the case study on competition is an example of a co-operation taking place through transgovernmental networks and the case study on consumer product safety features co-operation through dialogue.

A full case study is dedicated to transnational private regulation, which analyses the forms that private regulation takes and in particular the development of standard setting bodies and the growing recognition and adoption by countries of international standards.

The case study on transboundary water management illustrates co-operation through the use of specific negotiated agreements such as treaties and conventions. It also provides the example of a specific institution established to manage the co-operation – the International Commission for the Protection of the Rhine.

Table A.1. Case studies and IRC mechanisms

	Canada-U.S. RCC	Chemical safety	Consumer Product safety	Model tax Convention	Competition law enforcement	Trans-national private regulation	Trans-boundary water management	Prudential regulation of banks	EU Energy regulation	Global risk assessment dialogue
Integration/ harmonisation									√	
Specific negotiated agreements				√			√			
Regulatory partnerships between countries	√									
Membership in international organisations		√	√	√	√					
Mutual recognition agreements		√								
Transgovern-mental network					√			√	√	
Recognition of international standards						√				
Soft law		√		√	√					
Dialogue/ Exchange of information			√							√

Source: Based on the OECD IRC case studies.

The case study dealing with prudential regulation of banks illustrates regulatory co-operation through various global regulatory committees and networks.

The case study on EU Energy Regulation provides a focused example of regulatory co-operation taking place within the framework of the EU and involving both supranational elements and elements of transgovernmental regulatory networks.

The case study on the Global Risk Assessment Dialogue illustrates co-operation on an emerging issue via dialogue and exchange of information that aims, through international and collaborative working between members of the scientific community, at improving mutual understanding across jurisdictions and promoting consistency-specific methodological and substantive issues relating to risk assessment.

B. Analytical framework used to structure the information in the case studies

A common outline was developed to structure the material for case studies, in order to ensure some comparability of approach among case studies and that all important dimensions are covered. This outline follows.

Introduction: the context of IRC

Area where IRC is taking place – e.g. environment, chemicals, trade, financial services, energy –, sector specificities, socio-eco context underpinning the co-operation, what is the opportunity.

1. Main characteristics of the IRC under consideration

Actors involved: number and nature:

- Governmental:
    - Level of government: national, supra-national and/or sub-national;
    - Responsible authority: centre of government, line ministry, regulatory agency, etc…
- Non-Governmental – business, civil society

Intended objectives of IRC:

- market access, economic competitiveness;

- regulatory efficiency gains (reduce costs due to unnecessary differences in regulations and economies of scale);

- improve quality and effectiveness of regulation through exchange of information/access to good regulatory practices, tools, methodologies and networks;

- level the playing field and prevent regulatory arbitrage by setting minimum standards and regulatory alignment;

- facilitate operation of own regulatory regime when dealing with transboundary activities/phenomena (e.g. crossborder co-operation on investigations, management of global goods and bads);

- facilitate inter-operability of systems (e.g. common technical standards for transport, energy);

- conflict avoidance/resolution;

- build consumer/user trust.

Forms that the co-operation is taking:

- Formality – from voluntary to legally binding. A distinction could also be drawn between IRC mechanisms where law is created or harmonised and joint management of cross-border issues where no regulation is created but guidelines or other forms of "soft law" are produced.

- Scope – from partial to comprehensive

- Mode of co-ordination

  - hierarchical – one institution as clear leader setting standards others implement

  - bilateral/peer group – mutual recognition, MOUs; peer review

  - managed network – co-ordination on processes, practices, interoperability

  - market based – implementation through market operations;

- Instruments/tools of co-operation

  - Formal (umbrella type) regulatory co-operation partnerships with other countries (EU, Transatlantic Economic Partnership, Canada-U.S. Regulatory Cooperation Council…)

  - Membership in international organisations promoting regulatory co-operation (WTO, OECD, APEC…)

  - Area-specific legally binding agreements (Conventions, Protocols such as the Montreal protocol, OECD Council Decisions…)

  - Recognition of international standards, certification schemes and systems of conformity assessment

  - Mutual recognition agreements/Equivalence agreements

  - Formal sector-based co-operative agreements such as MOU, structured dialogue between regulators, etc.

  - Soft law: Peer review mechanisms, forums, guidelines, roadmap, etc.

  - Informal exchange of information

- Functions being co-ordinated/components covered in co-operation

  - *Ex ante* exchange of information

  - Agenda setting / setting goals / strategies

  - Formulating rules / norms / standards

  - Risk assessment

  - Monitoring, data collection

  - Supervision

  - Enforcement – imposition of sanctions, provision of incentives to comply

  - Crisis management

  - "Clean up" / responding to disasters which have cross-border dimensions

2. Short history of the development of the IRC

Triggers:

- proximity of issue;
- cross-border impacts of domestic regulations;
- management of cross-border risks;
- costs of non-co-operation;
- driving actors (business, etc.)

Time period, main landmarks

Institutional set-up: who does what in the co-operation, at what level of government

Next steps envisaged in the co-operation:

- new or forthcoming areas for co-operation – Emerging challenges
- involvement of new actors
- evolution of new modes and mechanisms of co-ordination

3. Assessment (quantified when available)

Benefits of existing IRC as it exists:

- economic efficiency gains,
- increased trade and investment flows,
- progress in managing risks across borders (in relation to the environment, health, safety, consumer protection or crime prevention) and avoiding global systemic risks (financial sector);
- greater transparency and work-sharing across governments and public authorities;
- more efficient administrative relations
- reduced costs on economic activity
- knowledge flow and peer learning

Challenges (and when they exist, mechanisms to overcome them):

- entrenched regulatory path/specificity of regulatory set up
- regulatory sovereignty
- unequal distribution of costs and benefits within and across countries
- regulatory competition (as a factor preventing co-operation or driving negotiations towards acquiring a competitive advantage for domestic institutions or companies)
- interpretation of "national interest"

Costs and financing:

- administrative costs of IRC infrastructure
- additional layer of co-ordination/regulation
- "race to the bottom": lower quality regulation

Scope for improvement

Conclusion: success or failure?

- Indicators/benchmarks against which IRC in this field is considered a success/a failure
    - Comprehensiveness: number of key players (countries and other stakeholders such as companies) which joined the agreement; coverage and exemptions
    - Level of compliance and credibility
    - Regulatory objectives reached
- Factors of success/failure
    - Possibility/easiness of evaluating impact and progress achieved through IRC
    - Leadership/champions
    - Compensation mechanism for losers/financial incentives for less developed countries

- Incentives for participation and compliance – how is free-riding addressed

- Feasibility of monitoring and detection of non-compliance

Annex B

The IRC survey

About International Regulatory Co-operation (IRC)

The OECD is currently exploring the manner and extent to which countries co-operate with one another in their regulatory activities. In this questionnaire, the term "regulation" is used to refer to all instruments by which governments set requirements on citizens and enterprises, and the associated activities of monitoring and enforcing those requirements. We define international regulatory co-operation (IRC) mechanisms as any agreement, formal or informal, between countries to promote some form of co-operation in the design, monitoring, enforcement, or *ex post* management of regulation. Mechanisms may run from voluntary to legally binding agreements, from partial to comprehensive arrangements and involve various modes of co-ordination. Typical mechanisms involve, but are not limited to, formal regulatory co-operation partnerships between countries, mutual recognition agreements, recognition of international standards and certification schemes, and memberships in international organisations promoting regulatory co-operation.

Aim of this questionnaire

The questions on IRC aim to support the OECD Secretariat in gathering information on institutional organisation of regulatory co-operation and intensity of use of a range of co-operation mechanisms. This information will complement lessons learnt from a selection of case studies and a survey of the literature.

A. Official definition and organisation

International regulatory co-operation is a new area of work for the OECD Regulatory Policy Committee, as well as for many OECD countries. This section explores the existence of definition and classification of international regulatory co-operation and gathers information on institutional organisation for regulatory co-operation.

---

*1. Does your government have an explicit, published policy or a law on international regulatory co-operation?

☐ Yes

☐ No

1a. If yes, please send via e-mail a copy of these documents. If they are not in English or French, please also provide us with a short summary in English.

```
Summary (if your policy or law is not in English)
```

1b. If yes, does this policy apply for all sectors?

☐ Yes

☐ No

1b1. If no, please list the sectors to which it applies:

```
```

*2. Does your country use a definition of international regulatory co-operation across all levels of government?

☐ Yes

☐ No

2a. If you answered yes, please provide us with this definition. If your definition is not in English or French, please also provide an English translation of the definition.

```
```

*3. Has your government developed or does your government use a classification to group the different international regulatory co-operation mechanisms?

▢ Yes

▢ No

3a. If yes, please provide us with that classification. If your classification is not in English or French, please also provide us with an English translation of the classification.

```
                                                                    ▲
                                                                    ▒
                                                                    ▒
                                                                    ▼
◄ █                                                                 ►
```

*4. Does your government keep a database or a list of all its international regulatory co-operation mechanisms currently in force?

▢ Yes, a central database exists.

▢ Yes, all line ministries or agencies maintain their own sector-specific databases.

▢ Yes, some line ministries or agencies maintain their own sector-specific databases.

▢ No, such a database does not exist.

4a. If yes, please provide the link if the list is publicly available online or attach this list. Please also provide us with a brief description of your methodology (i.e., how this list is compiled) and who is responsible for compiling the list.

```
                                                                    ▲
                                                                    ▒
                                                                    ▒
                                                                    ▼
◄ █                                                                 ►
```

*5. Is there a single central/federal government ministry or government agency in charge of international regulatory co-operation in general?

▢ Yes, a line ministry

▢ Yes, an agency

▢ No, this responsibility is shared amongst several central/federal government bodies.

☐ No, this responsibility is shared among sub-national and central government bodies.

☐ No institution is responsible.

☐ Other [   ]

5a. If yes, please provide us with the name and web link of this body or these bodies.

[   ]

*5b. Please briefly explain how the process of international regulatory co-operation is organised in your country (the levels of government and responsible authorities involved: line ministries; regulatory agencies; sub-national authorities, etc.).

[   ]

B. Use of IRC mechanisms

This section seeks to understand which international regulatory co-operation mechanisms are currently in force in your country and the frequency of their use.

---

*6. Is your country part of any institution with supra-national powers that produces regulation, other than the EU?

☐ Yes

☐ No

6a. If yes, please name this institution or these institutions.

[   ]

*7. Please list your country's memberships in international organisations promoting regulatory co-operation.
(An example of this mechanism is the membership in the World Trade Organization, the OECD, etc.)

*8. Please list the **formal** (umbrella type) **regulatory co-operation partnerships** with other countries in which your country participates.
(Formal regulatory co-operation partnerships are broad political agreements between countries aimed at promoting better quality regulation and minimising unnecessary regulatory divergences. Examples include the EU, Transatlantic Economic Partnership, Canada-U.S. Regulatory Cooperation Council, etc.)

*9. When developing regulatory measures, is there a formal cross-sectoral requirement to consider all relevant frameworks for co-operation in other jurisdictions in the same field?
If yes, please send the formal requirement documents by e-mail.

☐ Yes, there is a cross-sectoral requirement to exchange information about new regulatory initiatives.

☐ Yes, there is a cross-sectoral requirement to consult with counterpart agencies in other jurisdictions before taking action.

☐ No, there is no cross-sectoral requirement, but it is done in some sectors.

☐ No, there is no formal requirement.

10. Recognition and incorporation of international standards and certification schemes.
(We define this mechanism as the incorporation of international standards in legislative instruments by means of a reference to one or more standards or the replacement of entire text in the drafting of a code or regulation. Examples include references or adoption of text from ISO standard)

*10a. Is there a formal requirement to systematically consider recognition and incorporation of international standards and certification schemes when formulating new domestic standards or revising existing ones?
If yes, please send the formal requirement documents by e-mail.

☐ Yes, in all sectors

☐ Yes, in some sectors

☐ No

10b. If you answered yes to question 10a, is there a formal requirement to explain the rationale for diverting from international standards when country specific rules are proposed?
If yes, please send the formal requirements documents by email.

☐ Yes, in all sectors

☐ Yes, in some sectors

☐ No

10c. If there is no formal requirement to systematically consider recognition of international standards and certification schemes but this mechanism is still used, please describe under which circumstances *and* in which sectors your country uses it.

10d. If your country does not use this mechanism, please explain why.

10e. If available, please provide an estimate of your country's share of technical regulations that are equivalent to international standards. Please also describe your methodology (how you calculated this figure).

*11. Does your country have mutual recognition agreements with other countries?
(States party to mutual recognition agreements decide that they will recognise and uphold legal decisions taken by competent authorities in another Member State. Mutual recognition is a process which allows specifications (qualifications, product, etc.) gained in one country to be recognised in another country. Please note that if you are an EU country you do not need to include mutual recognition obligations towards other EU member states that arise from membership of the EU).

 Yes  No

11a. If you answered "yes", please indicate which sectors use this mechanism, the title of the agreements and the dates they were entered into.

11b. If you answered "no", please explain why this mechanism is not used.

*11c. How many mutual recognition agreements are used in your country? If you do not have the exact number, please provide an estimate.

*12. Does your country use other mechanisms for international regulatory co-operation? (Examples of other mechanisms may include information sharing for the purposes of regulatory monitoring, supervision or cross-border enforcement, procedures for joint-rule making / standard setting)

 Yes  No

12a. If yes, please explain the mechanism(s) and provide an example. Please also state how often and, when appropriate, in which sector(s) each mechanism is used.

	Type of mechanism (please state the name and briefly explain)	In which sectors is this mechanism used?	How often is it used (provide numbers when possible)?	Example(s), including dates they were entered into
1.				
2.				
3.				

C. Benefits and challenges

This section seeks to understand country perception of the benefits and challenges associated with international regulatory co-operation.

---

*13. Has your country undertaken any cost-benefit analysis of its international regulatory co-operation mechanisms?

☐ Yes, in all sectors

☐ Yes, in some sectors

☐ No

13a. If yes, please provide an example and, if possible, your methodology and related links or material.

*14. Based on your past experiences of regulatory co-operation, please indicate the importance of the following potential benefits of international regulatory co-operation for your country.

	Very important	Important	Not so important	Unimportant	Not applicable (please explain)	Comments
Reduced costs on economic activity	☐	☐	☐	☐	☐	
Increased trade and investment flows	☐	☐	☐	☐	☐	
Progress in managing risks across borders	☐	☐	☐	☐	☐	
Greater transparency	☐	☐	☐	☐	☐	
Work-sharing across governments (e.g. avoiding unnecessary duplication of tasks)	☐	☐	☐	☐	☐	
More efficient administrative relations (e. g. clearer and less contentious)	☐	☐	☐	☐	☐	
Other (please	☐	☐	☐	☐	☐	

*15. Based on your past experiences of regulatory co-operation, please indicate the importance of the following potential concerns raised by engaging in international regulatory co-operation.

	Very important	Impor-tant	Not so impor-tant	Unimpor-tant	Not applicable (please explain)	Comments
Lack of regulatory flexibility of your own and/or other countries	☐	☐	☐	☐	☐	
Reduced regulatory sovereignty of your own and/or other countries	☐	☐	☐	☐	☐	
Legal obstacles (such as restrictions on information sharing / confidentiality rules)	☐	☐	☐	☐	☐	
Unequal distribution of costs and benefits within and across countries	☐	☐	☐	☐	☐	
Reduced regulatory competition (e.g. acquiring competitive edge through differentiation)	☐	☐	☐	☐	☐	
Lower quality of regulations, caused by the difficulty to find an international agreement	☐	☐	☐	☐	☐	
Increased administrative costs of IRC infrastructure for your own country (e. g. additional personnel, direct funding contributions)	☐	☐	☐	☐	☐	

Costs of additional layer of co-ordination/ regulation on economic activity	☐	☐	☐	☐	☐	
Other (please	☐	☐	☐	☐	☐	

16. This question seeks to understand in which sectors or policy areas IRC works best and is most problematic.

* 16a. In which sector(s) or policy area(s) has IRC been most successful in your country? Please explain.

(Possible examples for sectors would be the environment, trade, ...)

* 16b. In what sector(s) or policy areas has IRC been most problematic? Please explain.

Additional comments to clarify any of your answers to questions 1-16.

Were all questions clear and straightforward to answer?

Glossary

International regulatory co-operation: for the purpose of this report, IRC is defined as any agreement or organisational arrangement, formal or informal, between countries (at the bilateral, regional or multilateral level) to promote some form of co-operation in the design, monitoring, enforcement, or *ex post* management of regulation. IRC is not restricted to its strict equivalence with international legal obligations, but also includes non-binding agreements and voluntary approaches. Consequently, IRC mechanisms may run from voluntary to legally binding agreements, from partial to comprehensive arrangements, and involve various modes of co-ordination. Typical mechanisms involve, but are not limited to, formal regulatory co-operation partnerships between countries, mutual recognition agreements, recognition of international standards and certification schemes, memberships in international organisations promoting regulatory co-operation within particular sectors or more broadly, at the regional or global level, and transnational co-operation across private regulators.

Comity: Horizontal, sovereign-state-to-sovereign-state legal principle whereby a country takes other countries' important interests into account while conducting its law enforcement activities, in return for reciprocal action.

Co-regulation: A system of shared regulatory responsibilities in which an industry association or professional group will assume some regulatory functions, such as surveillance and enforcement or setting of regulatory standards.

Economic integration: Freedom of exchange among countries and economies, and the consequential flows of goods, services, capital, technology, knowledge and people (Australia and New Zealand Productivity Commissions, 2012).

European Union (EU) law: EU laws (regulations, directives and decisions) take precedence over national law and are binding on national authorities (website of the European Commission: http://ec.europa.eu/eu_law/introduction/treaty_en.htm).

Regulations are the most direct form of EU law – as soon as they are passed, they have binding legal force throughout every Member State, on a par with national laws. National governments do not have to take action themselves to implement EU regulations. Regulations are passed either jointly by the EU Council and European Parliament, or by the Commission alone.

Directives lay down certain end results that must be achieved in every Member State. National authorities have to adapt their laws to meet these goals, but are free to decide how to do so. Directives may concern one or more Member States, or all of them.

Decisions are EU laws relating to specific cases. They can require authorities and individuals in Member States either do something or stop doing something, and can also confer rights on them. They come from the EU Council (sometimes jointly with the European Parliament) or the Commission.

Global regulation / globalised approaches to regulation: Approaches that provide a global framework of rules and/or standards as a platform for country-specific action (Levy, 2011).

Hard law: In the context of international law, hard law refers to legally binding documents such as treaties or international agreements, as well as customary laws, which create enforceable obligations and rights for countries (states) and other international entities.

Harmonisation: Co-operation between governments to make laws more uniform and coherent.

Intergovernmental organisation (IGO): An agency set up by two or more state governments to carry out projects and plans in common interest (Yearbook of International Organisations). IGOs are established by a formal instrument of agreement between the governments of nation states (treaty or charter), which also defines the intergovernmental organisation's goals. IGOs possess a permanent secretariat performing ongoing tasks.

Meta regulation / Meta regulator: Process of regulating the regulators/regulator of regulators.

Mutual recognition agreement: Principle of international law whereby States party to mutual recognition agreements recognise and uphold legal decisions taken by competent authorities in another Member State.

OECD Acts and other legal instruments: The OECD's governing body, the Council, has the power to adopt Decisions, Recommendations, and other legal instruments as the result of the substantive work carried out in the Organisation's Committees (OECD website: www.oecd.org/legal/oecdlegalinstruments-theacts.htm).

> **Decisions** are legally binding on all those Member countries which do not abstain at the time they are adopted. While they are not international treaties, they do entail the same kind of legal obligations as those subscribed to under international treaties. Members are obliged to implement Decisions and they must take the measures necessary for such implementation.

> **Recommendations** are not legally binding, but practice accords them great moral force as representing the political will of Member countries and there is an expectation that Member countries will do their utmost to fully implement a Recommendation. Thus, Member countries which do not intend to do implement a Recommendation usually abstain when it is adopted.

> **Declarations**: solemn texts setting out relatively precise policy commitments are subscribed to by the governments of Member countries. They are not formal Acts of the Organisation and are not intended to be legally binding, but they are noted by the OECD Council and their application is generally monitored by the responsible OECD body.

> **Arrangements and Understandings**: instruments, negotiated and adopted in the framework of the Organisation by some Member countries. They are not Acts of the Organisation and are not legally binding, but they are noted by the OECD Council and their implementation is monitored.

Regulation: Decisions and instruments implemented within the framework of public actions, directly or indirectly, to improve social welfare. Regulation includes laws and regulations but also administrative formalities, code of conduct, etc.

Regulators: Administrators in government departments and other agencies responsible for making and enforcing regulation.

Regulatory power: Power given to public authorities to adopt and enforce regulations.

Regulatory rapprochement: Reduction in practical differences between regulations from different jurisdictions, so that, as regulations come to resemble each other or to have equivalent effects, a more unified regulatory system takes shape (OECD, 1994).

Soft law: Co-operation based on instruments which are not legally binding, or whose binding force is somewhat "weaker" than that of traditional law, such as codes of conduct, guidelines, roadmaps, and peer reviews.

Standardisation: Activity of establishing, with regard to actual or potential problems, provisions for common and repeated use, aimed at the achievement of the optimum degree of order in a given context. In particular, the activity consists of the processes of formulating, issuing and implementing standards. Important benefits of standardisation are improvement of the suitability of products, processes and services for their intended purposes, prevention of barriers to trade and facilitation of technological co-operation (OECD, 1998).

Transnational private regulation (TPR): New body of rules, practices and processes, created primarily by private actors, firms, NGOs, independent experts like technical standard setters and epistemic communities, either exercising autonomous regulatory power or implementing delegated power, conferred by international law or by national legislation (Cafaggi, 2011).

Transgovernmental relations: Sets of direct interactions among sub-units of different governments that are not controlled or closely guided by the policies of the cabinets or chief executives of those governments (Keohane and Nye, 1974).

Transgovernmental (also known as transnational) **regulatory networks**: Regulatory co-operation based on loosely-structured, peer to peer ties developed through frequent interaction rather than formal negotiation involving specialised domestic officials (typically regulators) directly interacting with each other (for instance through structured dialogues or memorandum of understanding), often with minimal supervision by foreign ministries.

Unilateral co-ordination: Reducing regulatory differences by taking the regulatory settings of the other country into account when reforming one's own law or by unilaterally recognising the law of the other country.

Vertical and horizontal co-operation mechanisms: Vertical co-operation implies co-ordination across different levels of government, while horizontal co-operation implies co-ordination across similar levels of government.

ORGANISATION FOR ECONOMIC CO-OPERATION AND DEVELOPMENT

The OECD is a unique forum where governments work together to address the economic, social and environmental challenges of globalisation. The OECD is also at the forefront of efforts to understand and to help governments respond to new developments and concerns, such as corporate governance, the information economy and the challenges of an ageing population. The Organisation provides a setting where governments can compare policy experiences, seek answers to common problems, identify good practice and work to co-ordinate domestic and international policies.

The OECD member countries are: Australia, Austria, Belgium, Canada, Chile, the Czech Republic, Denmark, Estonia, Finland, France, Germany, Greece, Hungary, Iceland, Ireland, Israel, Italy, Japan, Korea, Luxembourg, Mexico, the Netherlands, New Zealand, Norway, Poland, Portugal, the Slovak Republic, Slovenia, Spain, Sweden, Switzerland, Turkey, the United Kingdom and the United States. The European Union takes part in the work of the OECD.

OECD Publishing disseminates widely the results of the Organisation's statistics gathering and research on economic, social and environmental issues, as well as the conventions, guidelines and standards agreed by its members.

OECD PUBLISHING, 2, rue André-Pascal, 75775 PARIS CEDEX 16
(42 2013 14 1 P) ISBN 978-92-64-19705-3 – No. 60647 2013-01